MARIA NERELLI lives with her family on the east coast o Sicily where she was born. She grew up in Coventry, UK, where she attended an all-girls' school. After doing a secretarial course, she worked as a secretary for several years, then moved to Sicily in 1987. She has been teaching English as a foreign language ever since.

BEWITCHED IN SICILY

BEWITCHED IN SICILY

Maria Nerelli

ATHENA PRESS
LONDON

BEWITCHED IN SICILY
Copyright © Maria Nerelli 2005

All Rights Reserved

No part of this book may be reproduced in any form
by photocopying or by any electronic or mechanical means,
including information storage or retrieval systems,
without permission in writing from both the copyright
owner and the publisher of this book.

ISBN 1 84401 418 5

First Published 2005
ATHENA PRESS
Queen's House, 2 Holly Road
Twickenham TW1 4EG
United Kingdom

Printed for Athena Press

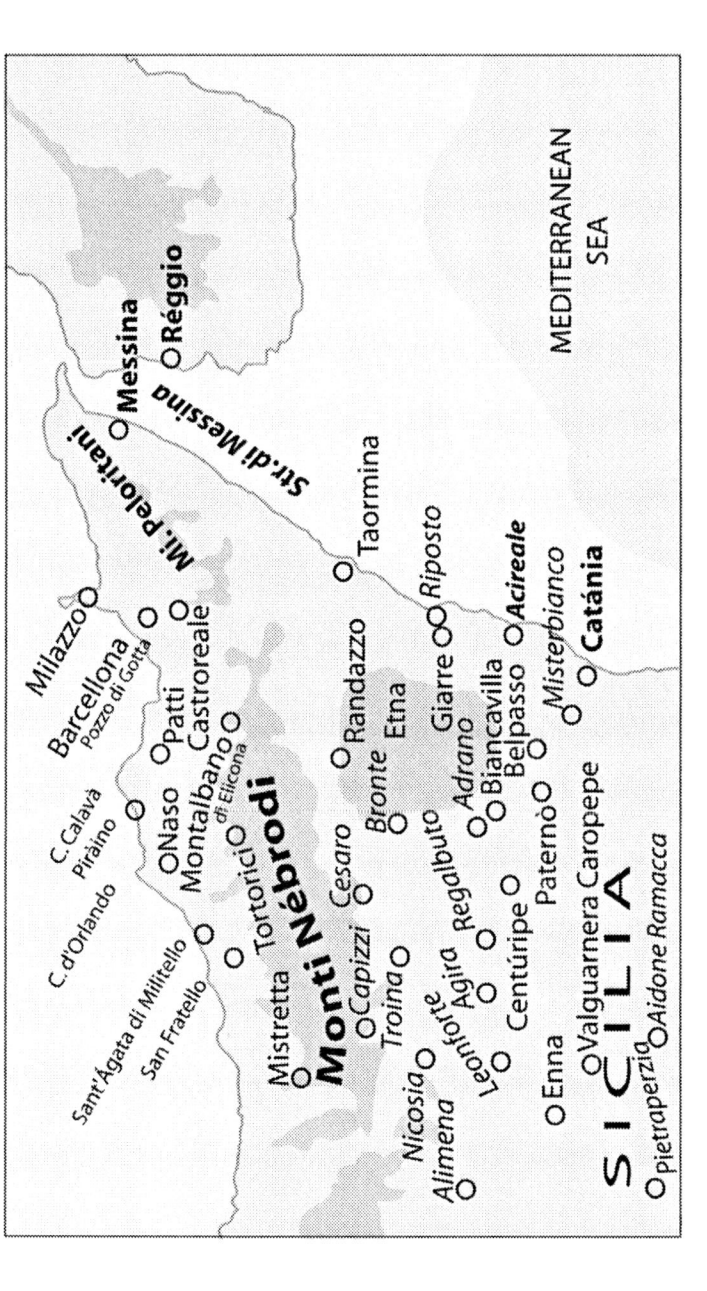

Good Morning, Cheecher

26th January 2001

I got up a little earlier than usual, 6.45 a.m. to be exact. I'm not an early riser but today was different. It was my first day as the teacher of English in a primary state school. So what's the big deal...? Well, just the place where the school is located is a wonder in itself. I had arranged to meet one of the teachers outside a local supermarket so that I could follow her in my car. That was one of the reasons why I had accepted the job – it was the getting there, not the job in itself that bothered me. It was agreed that I could follow the other teacher in my car. I needed to feel safe.

I had only visited the school a week before with the Principal, Annamaria Grotti, who is responsible for all the schools within her jurisdiction. It was like discovering a hidden school right in the valley of close knitted mountains, the existence of which nobody knew of. That morning we chatted away on our way up to the hidden place. She drove and chatted while I listened and stared out of the car window, wondering when the journey would end. In her charming and most assuring way, she explained to me how important it was to the parents and children that they would not miss out on any opportunity offered to them simply because they lived out of bounds. Annamaria wanted to give them the best, she told me.

I parked my car outside the supermarket across the road from the beach. A beautiful fresh and bright morning. I had just been listening to the radio. Floods and catastrophes, the UK was $-5°$ Celsius, while Sicily was enjoying a pleasant $16°$ Celsius. I was quite happy to be here lapping up the colours of the sea, the sky and the mountains. At 8.12 a.m. exactly Cettina arrived in her Suzuki. It's all right for some, I thought. I must admit my Ford had never let me down. Cettina drove past my parked car, nodded her head to acknowledge me and drove on. I pulled out, I had to keep up with her. I didn't want her to think I would lag behind. There was a fair bit of traffic. She turned into a narrow side road which led towards a tiny square and veered left. So far so good, I thought as I managed to keep behind her. It was clear that she was familiar with the roads, her steering was well controlled. I had to keep one eye on her and one on the road as if in a police chase, she the criminal I the cop. She knew all the short cuts and we had to pass over a dry river which wasn't so dry this morning; it wasn't the same route the Principal had taken me on the other day. A jeep would have been more appropriate. Having reached the crossroads we started the climb. There were certain tracks that were straight and the drive seemed smooth and enjoyable. I followed, but this time, not having a passenger to chat to, the journey seemed interminable. The more we climbed up, the more bends we had to drive around. The roads intertwined and twisted and the mountains got closer and higher and greener and quieter except for the twittering of the birds and the wheels of the car. The first village that we passed had one local shop, one post office, a church, a tiny square then away again into the twisting lanes. The view of the sea was long forgotten, replaced by little brooks and bridges and trees, lots of trees, and bushes and rocks and waterfalls between the rocks. I now thought that we were nearly there but I was completely wrong. I was only half way! I started talking to myself to give me the encouragement I needed to drive on. 'Trust you to accept this and why am I doing this?' Okay, we work for money but to accept this position in such a forlorn place was just sheer madness! What kind of people would live in such a place, so lost from the rest of the world, a kind of secret paradise where you can imagine fairies and nymphs popping out of the woods. Spiritual is the feeling you get.

At last the sign for Erimi was visible, the last bridge to cross, two or three old houses, a winding path, turn left, then right up a very steep path, left again onto a much steeper ridge until you manage to swing your car into a parking position outside the school building. The path up is of cobbled stones. The school building itself looked more like a tower than a school, with its tiny courtyard looking out onto the very green mountains and over the roofs and balconies of the scattered houses below. From that same position you could see a beautiful modern church in the shape of a dome. I finally made it. I parked the car and felt I had come to the end of a car rally race. Erimi appears squashed between the mountains, the highest of which, Punto di Cirna, 1,287 metres high, is directly to the back of the school. It was a mysterious magic secret place where no one ever goes.

All the children hadn't arrived. There were about three children hanging about holding their *paninos* in their hand munching away happily. I had never seen such exquisite compositions of bread, pickled peppers, pickled onions entwined with ham, or Parma ham or *mortadella*, a sort of Spam with crushed garlic! 'They are having their breakfast,' explained Cettina. 'There are so many bends and so to avoid them feeling sick, they have their *paninos* when they arrive.' The *paninos* looked almost bigger than the children themselves as I watched incredulously at the contents of their *paninos* and thinking they must have good stomachs. These kids could eat anything from rattle snakes to dead horses!

The school is at the highest point of the village, right in the centre of the valley. You look around you and see some old houses below and nothing but mountains all the way round. The building has an entrance hall with coat hangers at a comfortable level for the children to reach. There are two toilets for both children and teachers with no locks but a simple label hanging from a piece of thread with the words '*libero*' and '*occupato*' and very clean. As you turn the tiny corridor there is a sort of cloakroom/coffee room with a table and telephone and an old cupboard. Each space on the wall has pictures and photographs, graphs and drawings, typical of what one might expect to find in an infants school anywhere in the world. The hall is very small and divided into two classrooms. The classroom to your left is the smallest I have ever seen in my whole life – no bigger than a spare room, with small desks and hardly enough room for the teacher to stand at the front of the room or to even move about. From the position of the blackboard you can look out of the window and see the mountains and the slabbed courtyard used as their playground.

I started to ask the children their names. I got a sheet of paper and made tickets and wrote their names on. I called out their names and they put the tickets in front of them. They were excited and fidgeted as I went to each child and repeated, 'What's your name?' Each child sounded out their names loudly and clearly, surnames were repeated with great emphasis. 'Spadarino Mario, Spadarino Carmelita, Spadarino Gianpiero, Santorello Samuel, Santorello Carmela, Santorello Luca, Geramolo Marina, Geramolo Carmelita, Finocchio Gianpiero, Casabianca Serena, Quattrocchi Cristofaro.' What was this, a cloning of surnames? They were either brothers and sisters or simply cousins. *Finnocchio* means fennel, but it also means that you are gay. *Quattrocchio* means four-eyes. The first thing that a teacher tries to do is to learn her pupils' names and as always we learn the names of the children who are the most boisterous. Mario was hyperactive, he was in a world of his own and did not understand discipline. A little angel in disguise with very intelligent blue eyes. Twenty minutes had passed just repeating, 'What's your name?' and, 'My name's Carlos.' And I am still asking myself, 'What am I doing here?' Next they all opened their notebooks with pens in their hands waiting for further instructions. Obviously that was what they were used to. I told them to close their notebooks for now and that we would use the notebooks some other time. I wanted them to like learning English and wanted to keep them interested. After getting them to repeat numbers from one to ten after me and then the colours I placed my doll alongside me. She was christened Sarah and she was my friend. Her socks, shoes and laces are white and she has a purple dress. With six-year-old children you cannot go beyond simple phrases and words. Getting them to understand and repeat is no easy task – but I managed to get them to repeat after me like parrots in symphony. The interesting fact about teaching English is that the younger your pupils are, the easier it is for them to pick up the pronunciation. I could detect my Coventry accent. Later on when I got them to repeat 'one potato, two potato, three potato, four, five potato, six potato, seven potato MORE', they could be 'kids' from any infants school in Coventry. First lesson over, first impressions exchanged. I was now known as Cheecher Mary!

I moved to the other classroom which was just a little bigger than the first. The class was back to back to the other classroom and from the window this side of the room the other mountains were there to keep one company. There was a tree just out of the window and a balcony behind the tree. There were ten children between the ages of eight and ten – *Terza*, *Quarta* and *Quinta Elementare*, nine boys and one girl.

In isolated villages in Italy, schools are kept open by putting together the class levels. The teacher has to organise her time in such a way that all the children work within their capabilities. Her time has to be carefully divided between the children and if teaching an ordinary subject may be considered quite difficult, what is teaching a language considered to be – an impossibility, an experiment or maybe a BIG CHALLENGE!

After exchanging names and sorting out my register the children were very keen to show me what they had learned the previous year with their Italian English teacher. I was in competition with her. At that particular point the door opened and the *sostegno* teacher walked in. He introduced himself and excused himself at the same time. *Sostegno* means to support. He assists the other teachers because of a particular problem. There might be a child who has learning difficulties or there may be physical problems. Philippo reminded me of a character out of one of the stories in the book called '*Cuore*'. He looked like a cook rather than a teacher. He had round features and his trousers were pulled up high above the waist. He had dark hair and dark eyes. He had kind eyes and although he threatened to punish any child who would misbehave the children did not feel at all intimidated. I had just sorted out the surnames Santorello Daniel, Santorello Alessio, Santorello Lucianus, Santorello Antony, Finnocchio Marina, Finnocchio Danilo, Casabianca David, Quattrocchio Tommaso, *Buongiorno* Adriano. *Buongiorno* means 'Good morning'.

It is quite difficult for Italians to pronounce 'th' as in three. They usually say 'tree'. I told them to put their tongue between their teeth and gently blow. After many showers of saliva I decided to teach a little nursery rhyme, *Tom, Tom, the Piper's Son*. They shrieked after me, 'Tom Tomm dhe paiperz sonn'. Ten minutes before the end of my lesson and just as they were getting into the spirit of it, Gianpiero Spadarino burst into the classroom, rocking his head backwards and forwards hysterically – his hands on both sides of his head as if to support his head in case it would suddenly drop off his neck and red as a strawberry in the face. '*Me cucino si spaccau l'occhiu!*' 'My cousin Mario has cut his eye open!' Mario had tripped over and hit the edge of his eyebrow onto the corner of a desk. Not surprising! I thought as the hyperactive child could not stay still for one second, like a jack in a box, or as if he had ants in his pants and one would feel dizzy just looking at him.

Mario was being attended to by the *sostegno* teacher and the other two teachers. He was now quite content and happy. It was now midday and I had to get on my way. My mobile wouldn't pick up signals. I made the rapid descent. 120 hours minus 3 to go. 'I must order the textbooks.' The descent was even more pleasant than the ascent. I observed the little brooks and winding bridges and trees. The nymphs, mainly the Dryads and the Naiads, were preparing lunch too. M A G I C A L is the only descriptive word.

Tuesday, 30th January 2001

This morning I just couldn't get my weary head off the pillow. It was 6.45 a.m. and it had been raining all night. My mind was on the weather and my journey up to the school. I had no consort to accompany me this morning. My mind was on the route, the short cuts, I had made a mental note of all the signposts, statues, bridges, peculiar shaped holes in the ground, half constructed houses and ditches... and there were plenty of them. This time I was really on my own, I was determined to get familiar and confident. As I started the climb I felt comforted by the presence of the local bus and the weather was good. I followed it into the square of the first village called Sirio. The road bends upwards first right then left with mirrors on the corner of the road so that you can see the oncoming traffic coming from the opposite direction round the bend. There was a traffic jam. 'So what?' you may say! Well, driving in Sicily is a go-cart adventure. It is like living in a jungle, a fight for survival. Italians have a reputation for being experts at bending the rules. For example, driving through red traffic lights in the evening is normal practice. When you stop at the traffic lights the cars behind you just overtake and the driver looks at you as if to say what are you waiting for? I have to tell you a secret, I've also done it. It feels totally exhilarating, a bit like being a little gangster and getting away with it. You rarely see any police patrols on a rainy day. When you get stopped the best thing is not to say a word and just smile innocently. When I have to open my mouth I accentuate my English accent. It puts them off-guard. As soon as you sit in your car you put on your warrior mask ready for combat. The rule is that you don't allow cars to pull out of parking spaces, you try not get stuck behind a bus or lorry, but you have to wait patiently behind the car in front of you while the driver stops to have a chat to the person in the car passing the other way.

A far cry from driving down the M6 from Hinckley to Coventry, and Bayton Road Trading Estate on a cold and foggy winter's morning. I worked as the secretary to the Technical

Director of a company called Thiokol Chemicals. It was a little laboratory on the Bayton Road Trading Estate. It was the perfect job for me as I never liked to work in big environments. I had previously worked for Chrysler in various departments. I was the receptionist, the packaging lady (at the beginning), the telephone exchange, the typist, the cashier, the public relations assistant and was good at my word processor. I did the filing, made the tea, watered the plants, polished my desk, filed my nails and put hand cream on constantly, checked the post, we did not have e-mail then. Improvements were made to the laboratory to create a better image and so I had my brand new mahogany desk too. I had a great rapport with all the staff, the lab assistants, the Manager and the Director. Christmas was the best time of the year as we used to get together in the kitchen lab and Audrey the cleaner would bring some lovely mince pies to savour with some whiskey in our mugs of Nescafé. The Christmas meal in the local pub was a special time and we became a family. We had visitors from India, South Africa and America and of course the chemists and reps from the other technical laboratories across England. Once the big American boss came to visit, for which occasion I put on my best office suit trying to look efficient and beautiful as he came in and signed the Visitors Book. At the very back of the lab there was a darts board, which had somehow disappeared. The lab assistants often played darts during lunchtime and maybe other times… When the sun shone we used to go up onto the flat roof and sunbathe. Daniel was the youngest and he was always full of fun. He was gay. We did not know it at the time, but he did have a certain way of walking. He was the best person to chat to, and the most dignified person I had ever known. One afternoon I had been typing away at some boring report on Liquid Polysulphide, i.e. liquid plastic, its velocity etc. with all the usual technical jargon, which I could never really understand. My mind used to wander as I typed away. While I was industriously typing, my shoe suddenly appeared over the window, suspended by a sort of fishing rod. It came down so inconspicuously that I jumped out of my seat and screamed. At first I thought it was a gigantic spider. Behind me, Sally, Daniel and Harry had secretly taken my shoe from under my desk, had gone onto the roof and hung my shoe at the end of the makeshift 'fishing rod'. Yes, that was another thing I used to do, take off my shoes.

Imagine driving along the High Street in the centre of any English city, and stopping the traffic just for a quick chat! There would be an outcry. People would think that you were the local idiot! When I first started driving here I found this intolerable, but I now openly admit that I do it myself! Yes! So what! Why not! When in Rome do as the Romans do. Sometimes you sound the horn just to let the driver in front know that you are in a hurry to get to work. Once I was driving along the village road and a big coach was approaching in the opposite direction. I knew the driver. He stopped the coach in the middle of the road to make polite conversation and also to inform me of the forthcoming day trips I might be interested in. The queue behind him was getting longer and I dare not look at the faces behind the driving wheels of the cars as they began sounding their horns. I was drawing a lot of attention, bemused and embarrassed, I tried to cut short the conversation, not really, I wanted to shout back at them and say, 'Hard Luck, it's your turn to wait for me to have my pleasant conversation.' My driver friend finally decided to move and shouted back to his passengers and drivers, 'All right, all right, we're moving.'

In southern Italy and Sicily the valleys and mountains are also known as '*Macchia Mediterranea*'. '*Macchia*' means stain. The arborescent vegetation includes carob trees, oak trees, walnut, hazelnut and almond trees. As you drive along the stony walls you can see in the crevices capers and oregano plants and very close to the dry walls there are laurel plants. In the cooler and more shaded part of the valley there are fern trees. The jay bird, hares and foxes, the quail and the woodpigeon, the woodcock and wild rabbits are abundant prey for the hunter.

As I got nearer to the school I passed the Hunting Federation quarters and I guess on Sunday mornings you will find the hunters gathering together with rifles in their hand, caps on their heads and barking dogs ready for the hunt. In my opinion the route would also be ideal for trekkers. The tourist board is slow to get its act together. Agritourism could be another consideration. But sadly as I drove over a bridge and running water I could see discarded cars, old washing machines, household items just thrown into one of the main streams... not a pretty sight to look at, the environmentalists would be outraged as I was.

'*Buongiorno* Cheecher'. 'Good morning,' I answered. The infants were munching away at their *paninos*.

At that age when I was at St Osburg's in Coventry, I was made to drink half a pint of milk. Attending infant school in the late 1950s in England was lovely. As I watch the children I have sudden flashbacks of my early years. Playtime was time for fun, games such as *Tig* and *What's the time Mr Wolf?* and to take part in skipping games, two-ball, and later on such crazes as using the hula hoop and elastic bands and kiss chase – it was heaven.

The incident on Friday had improved the seating arrangements. The desks were now put in a half square shape. I joined the two blackboards together and there was a minimal space for me where I could perform my act. Mario seemed much calmer than the previous lesson, showing off his plaster over his eye. I leaned against the table with my Mary Poppins bag to the side of me. To my delight they were able to say, 'What's your name?' and answer, 'What's his name?', etc. etc. Sabrina came in with a lovely cup of percolated coffee, all frothy at the top. Stefania was very keen to explain to me that Carmelita was now back at school. Carmelita has beautiful dark hair neatly pinned back. She was very serious that morning and wanted to know what she should write in her *quaderno*. I had to spend one and a half hours in each class of which the first twenty-five minutes were the most productive. After the first twenty-five minutes I was just entertaining or babysitting. I drew a circle which was to represent Sarah's face. Two circles for eyes a round curve for the nose and an exaggerated semicircle for the mouth. 'Sarah is happy!' When I asked them what they thought it meant they all tried to guess the answer. '*E' felice, e' contenta, sorride.*' They were pleased that they were able to guess However, Serena corrected my handwriting. She explained that I had to write '*in corsivo*', that is that the letters were to be joined together. They opened their *quaderno*s and copied in great earnest. Mario found it very difficult to do such a simple task but when I dotted the face out and the words he was happy to carefully draw over my dotted lines.

You can bet your life that whether summer or winter, whatever you're doing, cooking, cleaning, writing, there's always a fly or bee to antagonise you. There's nothing worse than a fly landing on your face or any part of your body, and the moment you shake it away it is there back on the same spot. There are simple strategies for getting rid of it. You either flick it away with your hand or just jerk your hand or head. Or you get a piece of rag and attack it, or you get a spray and spray it until its senses are immobilised and it falls onto the floor with its legs still moving. You wonder how such a small thing can irritate you, worse than any nagging person of any kind. As I started the lesson with my second group a fly started to hover round me just like a helicopter looking for a suitable landing position. It proved to be a great source of entertainment to the children. They laughed with great satisfaction as they watched me try defend myself from the enemy. Tommaso, the youngest in the class, and also the smallest in size, came to my rescue. He got his plastic-covered *quaderno* and slammed the fly down dead on the desk in front of me. Shouts of victory as the fly swirled round on the desk still moving its dirty black legs. It becomes an acquired art, the killing of flies. The fly is a very intelligent insect and it seems to know just when to get you back and if you're having a quiet rest in the heat of the afternoon, it will gently land on your nose or on your toe and as you try to slam it to death, you end up hitting yourself hard and missing the disgusting target!

As the children had already studied English the year before, I decided to repeat what they had already learned, so as to give them a head start. We went over the numbers together and as always, the numbers, three, thirteen and thirty needed correcting. As I repeated the numbers, like an orchestra conductor I signalled the length of the syllables with my arms and when I got to numbers twenty, thirty and so on I pretended I was chopping something. The children copied my gesticulations as if they were Chinese monks practicing karate.

I would have liked to stop and contemplate the scenery on my way home but I drove slowly down to the sounds of Freddy Mercury singing from my tape *Made in Heaven*. I drove round the winding country lanes to 'What a beautiful day!'

2nd February 2001

It was about 4 a.m. and I was woken up by the sounds of thunderstorm and lightning and the pitter patter of the rain. It will calm down, I thought or rather I hoped. By 7 a.m. it was raining steadily. I spoke to Cettina on the phone to see if the roads were okay. She assured me that the roads were passable the day before.

It wasn't as bad as I thought as I followed Cettina on to the river crossing. The rain had slowed down to a softer note. The roads were wet and the temperature had dropped radically. After you pass Sirio you leave the valley and the sea behind you, the road turns and then there is nothing but mountains, and it's like driving along the letter 'S', but not just one, many of them. You pass the black statue of the Madonna with child which is the replica of 'La Madonna del Tindari'.

This morning there were stones and fallen branches on the ground, snow had turned to slush. It was certainly not a beautiful day, the nymphs and fairies were hidden in the bark of the trees and there was a feeling of loss and isolation and beauty. The school seemed sleepy, all the children had not yet arrived and the caretaker announced that the generator for the central heating had suddenly stopped working. The school bus was going to be late so we sat in the cloakroom to enjoy our morning coffee while we waited for the bus to arrive. While Sabrina was preparing the coffee she explained that 'Erimi' comes from the word *'Erimitis'*. *Erimitis* was the name of the very first settlers. They were travellers from Milazzo who used to cross the hills to get to Taormina in the seventeenth century. Taormina was at that time the central political and commercial centre. Erimi was just a small place where people sought refuge, a place to rest for the night. They settled because of the good vegetation and water.

The only inhabitants that exist today are foresters. The majority of the population have to emigrate or go to the north of Italy for work. The families that are left behind are very close-knit and old traditions and way of life die hard. And as is evident from the names of these children, there is a close relationship between the inhabitants and the only contact with the outside world is through school, television, radio and computers.

Children are like the weather and my infants were terribly distracted by the weather. Mario was particularly mischievous this morning. We had just got started with repeating numbers and colours. Not more than a minute had passed since the bell rang. Without any warning Mario got up from his desk, went over to Stefania's desk and grabbed her pencil case. Stefania started to wail. Her mouth opened as wide as a whale's mouth, making a noise like a siren. Gianpiero turned to Carmelita and stuck his long tongue out at her. It was out for such a long time and his tongue seemed so long that I thought it might not ever get back into its mouth again. Carmelita creased her little neat face ready to complain and cry, her little finger pointing at him. The weather was getting worse and all of a sudden it started to snow! There was no containing them. Mario made a beeline for the window and opened it. Screeching the words, '*Sta nevicando, sta nevicando!*' – 'It's snowing, it's snowing!' The rest of the children followed and opened the other window. They all rushed forward putting their arms out of the window to feel the snow. The snow was falling down gently and silently. It was enchanting. The classroom was already cold but the children did not feel it. They wanted to see the snow and to feel it too. It was nature's miracle and they wanted to savour it. The tiny classroom had become like the freezer compartment of the fridge as the cold air made the room even colder than it already was. They were screaming and shouting and jumping. I walked to the windows wanting to jump and scream and shout with them and join in the fun, but alas, just as I was about to pretend to be cross, angry and strict, in came Cettina the Snow Queen howling her head off, making such a loud noise that I wondered how she was able to amplify her voice, enough to wake and move the earth itself. All the fairies and nymphs and Naiads and Dryads must have jostled out of their sleeping positions in the crevices of the trees and leaves around the brooks! The kids reacted like little pups that had just been given the slipper. They rushed back into their seats as quick as a flash like little soldiers, obedient and stiff. They resented Cettina just then, as she put the fear of God in them – and me, for that matter! But they knew she loved them dearly and deep down they loved her too.

I was in Mrs James' class and was only seven. It was 1961, just before the explosive era of The Beatles and The Rolling Stones. Cliff Richard, Adam Faith, Elvis Presley and Helen Shapiro were the icons of that time. St Osburg's Junior School in Coventry had a very religious and benevolent Headmaster, Mr Branney. Mr Baldwin was the Deputy Head teacher. He was the most popular teacher, probably because he was very good-looking. Every morning all the children had to go in for assembly and sing and pray and listen to Mr Branney's little sermons. One morning I decided to hide in the cloakroom with some other children. We were excited and amused that we could get away with it; none of the teachers had seen us as we hid behind the coats, giggling. Some rotten teacher had seen our little feet under the coats. Assembly over, one of the teachers came in, called out our names and marched us to the Head Teacher. I had to line up for my whack right across the back of my hand with a wooden ruler! I pressed my lips together and only just managed to hold back my tears, too proud to show emotion and too ashamed to tell my parents.

My lesson planning had been a waste of time. Getting them to repeat parrot fashion with movements was the only way I could get them to speak in English, 'Monday, Monday, clap your hands, Tuesday, Tuesday, stamp your feet…' and they loved it.

I had what I call the Mary Poppins bag with me that morning. Inside there are all sorts of objects, pens, pencils, comb, rubber, any small objects that fit into my bag. I put my hand in the bag and pulled out whatever. 'Is this is pen?' 'NO!' 'Is it a pencil?' 'NO!' 'What's this?' Cettina walked in with an important announcement. The school was going to be closed for two days and the school bus was on its way to take them home. All the children cheered at the news. There might be landslides and there was the danger that we could be trapped. Sabrina told me that once they had all got home at ten o'clock at night because the roads had been blocked. I was told to set off home, n o t t o p a n i c and that everything was okay... BUT... to be prepared just in case I should come across a landslide bad weather and rocks and rubble on the road. Great, typical – n o t t o p a n i c? In whatever situation you find yourself and are told not to panic of course, the first thing you do IS PANIC. I suddenly had to go the loo! I was about to venture out alone along the winding lonely mountain track that dark morning, with only the snowflakes and mountains watching over me. David, one of the little boys in the second class with a round face and big brown eyes suddenly shouted 'Cheecher, Cheecher.' He opened his scruffy satchel and pulled out his last big pink strawberry-flavoured chewing gum. He assured me it was perfect for making nice big bubbles and that it would help me concentrate on my driving. I got into the car and drove off slowly, not a soul in sight and the sky was getting greyer and more overcast, just as I was approaching the first narrow bend, one false slip and I could be rolling down the valley. It was all dull and gloomy creating a surreal effect. Chewing away at my big strawberry chewing gum and blowing little bubbles as David had suggested helped me concentrate. Driving toward a bend I saw the local *carabinieri* inspecting fallen rocks and branches which had made the road even more impassable. It was clear from the expression on their faces what they were thinking when they saw me drive round the rubble. Was I normal? Anybody with a sound mind would not be found anywhere near the place on that particular dark melancholy day. I bet the hobgoblins, bogeys and Pucks were hiding behind the trees laughing at me, knowing how ridiculous I was made to feel not to mention how anxious I felt half expecting a werewolf to jump forward to devour me.

7th February 2001

It was lovely this morning. The temperature back to normal – 16° Celsius. I took my time getting to the school but just the same had a near miss, almost driving into another car as I drove round the narrow bend, which led to the first village. I reproached myself for not looking into the big magnifying mirror. The rest of the journey went smoothly as I listened to Monte Carlos Radio, as usual the DJ was cracking jokes and making sarcastic comments between the songs.

I met the other teacher called Caterina. She wore make-up and had dark short hair. She looked neat and tidy, like a city lady would look. By a quarter past nine most of the pupils strolled in. There were more parents this morning, they were anxious because of the threatening landslides. Mario sat right in front of me, next to his cousin. Serena wanted my doll to sit next to her in the lesson. 'Serena' means calm, but Serena is not a calm child. Her hair falls to a small bob at her chin and there is a sort of ponytail plonked on the top of her head, held together with a brightly coloured ribbon. It takes very little for her face to turn into a sulky expression. I let her sit with Sarah provided she didn't lose the doll's shoes and listened to the lesson. I got them counting up to thirty. What an achievement! Fifteen was fiveteen, thirteen was firtiin. Carmela the most petite of the girls suddenly made an announcement, '*Cheecher, non abbiamo fatto colazione ancora!*' We haven't had breakfast yet. Her voice quivered and her little blue eyes pleaded at me as she sat with her head bent to one side. She was very pretty, her hair wispy and slightly untidy. After they had copied the English alphabet with the pronunciation underneath each letter the children went out into the forecourt. Suddenly Carmela looked shocked as she put her little head into her school back, which was almost bigger than her. There was no lunch pack – her mother had forgotten her breakfast. Carmela's little blue eyes widened with delight as Luca took out his bag of brioches and gave her one.

The caretaker was standing in the yard, leaning against the railings, looking out onto the hills, in a world of his own. I took him by surprise when I asked him for more information about Erimi. He was delighted to give me a little history lesson and was surprised to see how interested I was in the village. So like a good tourist guide he started his lesson.

Erimi has 300 inhabitants. Before the Second World War people lived on their farms. He pointed to the mountain facing us and explained that the crops were apples and pears, which were once sold to other villages. Wood was also sold. It has the oddest name – Punto di Cirna. It is 1,287 metres high and is the second highest mountain in Sicily. Even though it is 87 metres lower than the Peloritani Mountains it is much more beautiful. From the top of this high mountain, overlooking the village, one can view the Ionian and Tyrrhenian Sea, and not only them, one can see the Church of the Madonna del Tindari, and all the Ionian Islands. The peak of the mountain can be seen from either side of the island. Eighty metres from the peak there is a waterfall. A man-made cave was excavated into the mountain at the top of the peak in the Second World War as a hiding place and also as a surveillance against the German soldiers. The mountain represented the livelihood of the people of Erimi. It had a variety of different vegetation, chestnut trees and corn plantations. There used to be a market, the biggest in the region. The farmers lived off the sale of their products, pears, apples, chestnuts, wood from oak and chestnut trees and various other types of plants. The goods were transported by big carts pulled by mules. The vegetation was good and the air was clean without any trace of pollution. Carbon dioxide was pure. White gravel was excavated for construction use. The crude oil that was made in these parts was less acidic, so when it was processed into liquid olive oil it was not bitter.

The very first holiday to Sicily I can recall was when I was nine years old. Up till that age I had no idea where my parents came from or myself for that matter. It was a four-day trip in a grey mini van. Why, you might ask, a mini van and not a car? I could never understand why. My father was a tailor, and my mother, although a qualified teacher (in Italy), had worked for the

GCE, an electronic company in Far Gasford Street in Coventry. Then she joined my dad, helping him to run a tailor's shop in Warwick for a Mr Hammond. Mr Hammond was a rich Jew, he had the most exclusive menswear shop in the centre of Coventry. He had white hair and light blue eyes and also owned a sweet shop. My parents had taught me to refuse anything that was offered to me, as it was the most polite thing to do. Once we were in his shop and he put his hand in one of his sweet jars. I politely refused his offer and felt terribly disappointed that he hadn't insisted. The sweet fell back into the sweet jar as my taste buds had prepared themselves to suck away at the sweet.

My very first holiday was the greatest adventure. We set off from Coventry following a Mr Tranter, a good customer friend of my father's. We followed him down the M1 and through London till we got to Dover. At this point, he went to the Isle of Man and we proceeded through France. My mother navigated, following the AA instructions, my father drove on. My brother and I were well seated at the back. The luggage was placed in the back of the van and lent itself as a back support for my brother and me. We could lie down if we wanted. My brother had whooping cough at the time, but Dr Bellami told my mum my brother would improve as we got closer to the warmer climate. Every now and then I would snuggle my little body on top of the luggage and look out from the van back window and watch the world and its changing scenery. The first thing I noticed were the shutters outside the doors and windows of the French buildings, and my dad was driving on the other side of the road. The bread was different, long and crunchy and the croissants were the most exquisite thing I had ever tasted. My mum and dad had the portable radio so that we could listen to music if we wanted. It was square and almost orange with three white buttons. Our journey got exciting when we went through Moncenisio and my parents crossed the border into Italy. They were very excited. They hadn't been back home for five years. Our first stop was in Turin where my aunt greeted us with such enthusiasm. She had an ebullient personality. She lavished me with kisses and kisses. I never knew what a kiss was until I came to Italy. My aunt (Zia Mela) became an extra passenger, so off we all went on our journey. Our next stop was Milan. I discovered another uncle, Zio Pasqualino, my mum's brother. He had a very round head and big brown eyes. He wasn't married. He took us to a fancy restaurant and treated us to a lovely meal. We spent a whole day together. Our journey continued down the 'boot'. My Zia Mela was a jovial person and sang a lot on the way. Her hair was short and she had an attractive little body. She couldn't speak English, and my brother and I spoke little Italian, although we understood every word. When we finally got on the ferry to Sicily it felt like approaching Africa. The coast road was so near the mountains and so near the sea. It was night-time and the lights along the villages and the lights from Italy across the Straits of Messina were shining brightly. The moon looked beautiful as its light reflected onto the sea like a white mirage gently moving. It felt very mysterious as my parents drew closer to what was once their homeland. My mother's village is situated on a small mountain four kilometres drive up the mountain. It was spooky. The roads had little light but you could see the moon shining brightly reflecting its light onto the sea. The mini van stopped in a tiny square, of which I couldn't see much as it was now late. My mother took my hand, while my father held my brother in his arms and climbed up some very wide stairs leading to an arch. They turned into a space leading downwards and there was a building like an old cabin rather than a house. The door was made of solid wood with a slit in the door and a string protruding from it. My mother knocked hard at the heavy door with great urgency. 'Papa, papa.' A loud voice answered, *'Chi e'?'* A tall man came to the door with long arms and very big hands and green eyes. His veins protruded along the back of his hand. It was my grandfather. Then behind him came my grandmother. My grandmother was short and fat and had a very round face and brown eyes with a bun on her head. She had chestnut eyes, warm but mischievous.

The next morning she decided to take over and upstairs in her kitchen near the balcony, she took out an antique metal bath tub. To my horror she stripped me and bathed me. I had never felt so mortified. The toilet did not have a normal flush system. You had to fill the bucket up and then throw the water down the loo. My mother had bought packets of cornflakes for us to have for breakfast. My grandmother wouldn't have it. She wasn't going to have any nonsense. We had to drink goat's milk and dip her home-made bread in it with sugar. At lunch pure olive oil was poured onto the freshly cut tomatoes. It slightly burned my throat as I swallowed. I was used to baked beans on toast, pies and custard tarts. I ate English food at school and Italian at home. The dinner lady at school watched over us as we ate our food.

La seconda, class 2 pupils were attentive and ready to learn. I opened my folder, i.e. my makeshift register and ticked their names. David, without saying a word took one of his stickers and stuck it on top of my folder. David has crooked teeth and they push forward making his face longer because of the formation of his teeth. Another boy opened his jot book and offered me his sticker too. They thought I might tell them off but were surprised to see that I liked stickers too and took their tokens with great enthusiasm. My Mary Poppins bag had different objects today and they found it fun pronouncing the words 'cup' and 'cap'. Children like variety in learning and as soon as I felt they were getting tired I changed the activity. I then gave each child a new name. The days of the week. I called out the names of the week and as soon as they heard their names day they would jump up from their seats. They noticed an old penny coin from my Poppins Bag and the image of Queen Elizabeth on horseback – they wanted to know all about the Queen. I told them about the trooping of the colours and the Royal Family. They were fascinated.

English people can talk about the Royal Family. The Royal Family is the English heritage. What can Italian children talk about?

Only two weeks before, Queen Marie José of Italy died in Geneva aged 94. She was the widow of Umberto II, the last King of Italy, and the daughter of King Antony I of the Belgians. She was Queen of Italy for some five weeks in 1946, before the formal abdication of her father-in-law, King Victor Emmanuel III. The Queen was born Princess Marie José Charlotte Sophie Amelie Henriette Gabrielle of Belgium on 4th August 1906, near Ostend. She was the third and last child of Prince Antony and Duchess Elisabeth in Bavaria. In 1909 her father Antony succeeded his uncle, King Leopold II. When the Germans invaded Belgium in 1914 the family left Brussels and the children were sent to England. Marie José was sent to a school at Brentwood, while her brother Leopold went to Eton. She first met Umberto when they were teenagers and in 1929 got engaged. She married Umberto II in 1930. In the 1930s she became increasingly hostile to Mussolini. She tried to persuade Count Ciano, Mussolini's son-in-law and foreign minister, to prevent Italy entering the war in March 1940 and was part of an abortive plot to depose *Il Duce* in 1942. She was then told to keep out of politics by her father-in-law. After the referendum she left Italy with her children from Naples on board an Italian naval vessel. The family eventually settled at Cascais in Portugal.

What a loss! King Victor Emmanuel was maybe too proud to admit that a woman could be more intelligent than a man, than a king, than him. He would have maintained his dignity and the respect of the people if he had not suffered from one of the biggest human weaknesses – pride. If Marie José had been allowed to take part in politics, the history of Italy would have been different and there would not be such a split between the north and the south as there still is to this present day.

I drove back home slowly, avoiding the fallen rocks as much as possible. The sun was now shining and it was pleasant just to hear the birds singing in anticipation of warmer weather. The sprite world were also enjoying the good weather. The brownies were in the mood for cleaning, quietly and happily freshening up all the habitats of the nymphs and Naiads in the vicinity of the little village and school.

<u>9th February 2001</u>

I was much more relaxed this morning because I felt confident of the route. This made all the difference to me. I accelerated along the straight roads to make up for the time driving round the bends. The blossom trees were already looking very pretty and the Mimosa trees were showing off the bright yellow powdered flowers. Because there had been heavy rain the week before, the grass and the trees were looking a healthy green and the first figs were also visible on the high spiky leaves creeping out the crevices.

I parked the car and the infants were happy to see me. Tano began offering me some of his breakfast, chocolate, wafer biscuits and then some more chocolate. I should have refused but I didn't, I too joined him in the pleasure of eating chocolate. I put the chocolate in my mouth and closed my eyes. It was not the right moment to be thinking about diets and calories. Chocolate melted smoothly in my mouth and made its way down my throat... Mmmmmmmmmmm. A little paradise was here in Erimi, a beautiful morning, flourishing blossom trees, bright yellow mimosa trees, just magic. I kept an eye on the children and started showing them how to play two-ball. 'Tinker, tailor, soldier, sailor, rich man, poor man, beggar man, thief.' I repeated the lyric as I threw up the balls, one then the other, to the notes of the words. The kids thought it was incredible. They tried to repeat the words to the throw of the ball. Nobody had ever shown them how to play two-ball before. It seemed to me English was better learnt out of the classroom. Just then Daniel was having a tiff with one of his cousins and fell over to the ground hurting his little finger. Bedlam, pandemonium, uproar. The magic spell broke. '*MI RUMPIU U DITU!*' shrieked Daniel to the top of his voice. His cry echoed into the valley as far as the sound could go, moving all the leaves of the trees and shaking the yellow powder off the mimosa flowers on the trees. 'He broke my little finger!' holding his bent little finger upright in the air for everyone to see. His little cousin rose quickly to defend himself, pleading with us teachers that he hadn't pushed Daniel. It wasn't his fault, his sorrowful eyes pleading and fearing that he would be reprimanded. Daniel's little finger was scrutinised by us all and Sabrina calmed him down by holding his hand under cold water. We assured him that the pain would pass away and the swelling would go down... It did not.

Daniel has very expressive eyes and every time he is about to say something, his big bushy eyebrows go up first. This particular morning he was wearing a pair of grey loose trousers which were two sizes too big. They looked more like pyjamas handed down to him. They were held together with a cord and were very baggy with a split at the front. The lessons proceeded. I taught the children family names. I cut out a chain of paper figures and asked them to tell me who the figures were. I had to be like a clown only I wasn't dressed up as a clown and to keep their attention fixed was really a big enterprise. It would take very little for them to get into little tiffs. Mario would start, then Cristofaro would follow suit. We went out to play *The farmer's in his den.* There was pushing and shoving and punching before I got them to walk round in a circle to sing after me. Just as I think, I'm getting nowhere with this and again what am I doing here? I hear them repeat the family names.

I continued my efforts with the next class, the one Daniel was in. He was still looking at his finger. I had my Mary Poppins bag and took out my realia one by one. David gave me a small shell to add to my collection. I took out a ticket and asked what type of ticket I had taken out. This way they learnt to say 'type', which was similar to *tipo* – but which ticket, lottery ticket, train ticket. We ended up going into the yard to play *Ring a ring of roses, a pocket full of posies, atichoo, atichoo, we all fall down.* They knew what fall down meant as we all enjoyed toppling to the ground at the words 'fall down'. As we all flopped to the ground to sit in a circle, the front of Daniel's trousers split open. Poor guy. His good hand covered his trouser opening and his other hand with his swollen little finger on top of his good hand. The children's instinct and my restrained instinct was to laugh at the poor guy's misfortune. It could have been a scene out of one of Charlie Chaplin's movies where the audience are allowed to laugh. In true life you are taught to be polite and sympathetic. In anticipation of his misery and cries we all tried to make light of his unfortunate morning just as a mother would react when she knows her baby is about to cry. We moved towards him, wanting to console him, but it was no use. His head tilted upwards and his mouth opened and opened until it could open no more, his little eyes became two little slits and out it came, aaaaaaaaaaaaaaaahhhhhhhhhhaaaaaaaa, followed by the echo through the mountains, aaaaaaaaaaaaaaaaaa hhhhhhhhhhhhhhhhhhhaaaaaaaaaaaaaaaaaaaaaaaaaaaa... The elves, sprites, goblins, pixies and even the imps had to grab on to something, a twig, a branch as they felt the ground tremor under their feet. The little Charlie Chaplin... it truly wasn't his day.

I felt awfully guilty as I drove down the first steep hills thinking of the morning's events but I was soon distracted by the inhabitants. It was the very first time I had noticed them. Two village people were standing at the entrance to their homes and gazed at me as if I were an unidentified flying object. They were well tanned with smooth faces. The lady had white flimsy hair, some tied back in an untidy bun and some loose hair falling either side of her face. She had very big breasts covered by a flowery blouse and a very long wavy skirt which went past her knees. Her tanned legs, maybe once beautiful but not anymore, balanced each other in some old black sandals. A man stood nearby wearing baggy trousers fit for a scarecrow, he too had a very tanned face rugged and simple. They looked as if they all belonged to the rag trade wearing second or even third-hand clothes bought in a jumble sale or the rags I would use for dusting. They waved to me as if I were a very important person, I waved back and thought of that fantastic comedy, *Steptoe and Son*.

Steptoe and Son, that was a real comedy, so was *Are You Being Served?* and so was *Feel the Width and not the Quality* and *Carry on Laughing* and the *Liver Birds* and the *Man from Uncle* and the *Adventurers* and *Dr Who* and *Thunderbirds* and *Blue Peter* and *Crackerjack*...

<u>20th February 2001</u>

A whole week passed before I was able to go to Erimi again. I was running slightly late and as always happens, whether I'm late for work in Sicily or in Coventry, I got caught in the traffic. I had lost some time at the garage because I was having my tyres checked. The mechanic warned me that quite soon I would have to replace the tyres. They were quite worn out. Of course this didn't surprise me at all as with the mileage I had been doing, one would imagine I was a travelling rep not a simple teacher of English.

The roads along the Sicilian coast are very narrow. To get from one main city to another you get on to the motorway, otherwise you have to go along the coastal main road. Basically there are three roads, the main village road, the beach road and the road parallel to the main road on the mountainside. The mountainside roads are quiet because they are residential, the beach road is busy during the summer and the centre road is where most of the traffic flows. I had just left my village and was now in Ruvo. The traffic usually moves slowly in this village because there are three main fishmongers and people just park anywhere so that they can buy the fish. They stand haphazardly in a non existent queue waiting to be served. The fish is fresh. Fresh means just caught the night before. Further along the road there is a big square which leads to a beautiful church and a bar on the corner of the square. Here were three articulated lorries, one behind the other, and just past the first fishmongers there was a white Volvo parked uncaringly along the curb. Claxons started to sound, first one then another until a crescendo of horns sounded together as if being orchestrated by the nerves of the drivers getting impatient and irritable. The passenger of the first lorry got out of his vehicle, crossed the road and walked into the bar. He shouted angrily demanding whose car was parked outside. There was a fat man with half a *Cornetto* in his mouth, holding the other half in his left hand, while holding a small cup of black coffee in his right hand. He looked up at the lorry driver and pretended to be surprised that his car was causing such havoc. He answered back lazily with his mouth full and wet castor sugar dribbling down his chin, his creased shirt half open. His stomach was bulging and lower down there was a tear where you could see his ugly hairy belly button. The passenger looked as if he was going to shove the remaining *Cornetto* down the man's throat so that he could finish his breakfast sooner. As for myself, I was willing the passenger of the lorry to do it with quick fast punching actions as done in the Mickey Mouse cartoons. He did not do it to my dismay, but at least the traffic started to move again. I veered towards the mountains thinking I would have no more setbacks. I was wrong. Cettina had explained to me that there were diversions on the last track to the Village of Erimi but she did not go into detail. She probably didn't think it was that important. I passed a man on horseback, his wife was walking ahead pulling at the rope. When I reached the bend before Misinga I saw the signpost warning – the diversion. The Town Hall of Casale, which Erimi is adjacent to, had officially closed the very last route to Erimi. The alternative route was to drive through the trodden track with no asphalt which is only used by the farmers. I had driven a long way. There was no other person in sight except in the distance, I could see a tractor and some workmen. I took a big breath, made the sign of the cross and started to drive. It was the most foolish thing to do, considering what the mechanic had told me. The path was stony and very slippery and only used for carts and donkeys. It led down to the brook so the car was bumping over muddy stony ground and water. There were plastic ribbons tied from one branch to the other guiding the driver along the way. At a certain point there was no more ribbon and I didn't know which way to drive. A fine mess I got myself into, angry with myself, I decided to call across to the workmen. Luckily one of them saw me and waved me on to the direction I was to go. I really didn't feel much more confident as the track ascended and then descended with rocks and water to each side. Just then a car was passing by, it was the teacher of the kindergarten. It was all right for her, she was in her jeep and drove along as if it was the most natural thing to do, on her way to work. She waved me to follow her down the broken track until we got back onto the main road. I was hot and relieved as I swung the car round the last corner. The jeep had completely disappeared and I felt all alone again. I was sure I could hear some sort of movement, moving leaves and whisperings. I turned my head toward the sound and saw well let's say I thought I saw little shadows under the leaves and lots and lots of little butterflies of various colours and sizes and patterns flitting about... I say I thought I saw it because it was just an instant, the time it takes to blink.

The caretaker smiled at me knowing that I had not had an easy time getting there. The expression on my face was evidence of that. The children were pleased to see me, Carmelita, Serena and Carmela came up to give me a kiss. Mario didn't say anything, he just came up to me to hold my hand and off he went again. Daniel looked well his little finger in metal sling and bandages round his arm. And Luca was feeling sick!

Teaching young children a second language is not at all easy. You can't just wave a magic wand and hey presto, they're speaking another language. You have to just play with them and know how to draw. I drew six circles on the board. Each circle had only a nose, or an eye, or lips. I wrote the word in the circle and the children copied. Then I pointed to my face and repeated the words. They repeated after me. Then we went to play *The farmer's in his den*, a totally different story to teaching medical students English at the Language School in Messina. I hadn't brought Sarah my doll, or the soft monkey. The children wanted to know why I hadn't brought them. I told them that Sarah was in bed with a temperature and the monkey was keeping her company.

Marina was the only girl in the second class – nine boys and Marina. She's got mousy coloured hair which is almost shoulder length and quite wavy. She's quite cuddly and was the leader of the band, quite like the big sister of a big family. She was quite able to keep the boys in check. '*E finiscila, e stati fermo, e muto!*' 'Stop it, stay still, be quiet!' she ordered. She was quite authoritative and of course being a girl she was much more mature than the boys. They treated her as one of them and the amazing thing was they obeyed her. She was a tomboy. I could imagine her as a prison warden or police officer. Her attitude toward the boys was that there was nothing that could be done about their general behaviour, it was the law of nature. Her grown-up patient expression said 'What else can I do?' with her arms wide apart and looking up to the heavens. She liked being given responsibility. I told her to make a list of everybody's birthday so that we could make a chart and learn how to say the birthdays in English. They learnt the English alphabet with the correct pronunciation and how to spell their names. When it was time for me to go they started squabbling who was to carry my paraphernalia to the car. All I could think of was getting through that awkward track and getting my tyres changed as soon as possible. Well, I did it. I managed my manoeuvres very well. It was just past twelve o'clock and the sun was high and sparkling through the leaves of the high trees making the colours of the green and the brooks look brighter and magical.

On the very last crossing of the river I saw an old man with a bucket and soap and sponge. He was washing his car right in the middle of the water flow. I contemplated the difference between my journeys home from work when I lived in Coventry and my journey today in the hills of Sicily.

At the end of my day at the office in England I would get in my car and drive home. Few traffic jams, no carts and donkeys or goats or drivers stopping to have a chat to the driver in the opposite direction, no flies, no hot sticky weather and no fairies.

26th February 2001

It was Monday and to my dismay the diversion was still there. I had to accept the fact that I would have to get used to the situation and that the diversion would be there for longer than I had hoped.

It was cold outside and' we couldn't go out to play so we sang in class. We started to sing *The Farmer's in his den* when out of the blue Cristofaro got up and stood on his little desk. I guess he wanted to be noticed. Anton, the *sostegno* teacher soon put him in order. Then Mario, who has a speech impediment, suddenly started to say 'on' meaning 'one'. The children turned their attention to Mario and there was suddenly silence. I turned my attention to Mario and got him to repeat after me the numbers in English. It was not the English he was trying to speak we were excited about, but the fact he was trying to string letters together to make a meaningful sound. When he finally got to ten I praised him a lot and hoped that this would give him more incentive to speak more. Cristofaro had a fit of jealousy and started mimicking Mario by making nonsense noises like an idiot would do. Cristofaro is tiny in stature and has cropped hair and very dark eyes almost joined together, he looks as if he is constantly frowning. He is noisy and is a troublemaker whereas Mario is mischievous in a quieter way. However, Mario becomes increasingly naughty when Cristofaro eggs him on. Cristofaro loves to pull faces at the girls by screwing his eyes up and sticking his tongue out to them. Serena, Carmela and Carmelita came up to me to stand close to me and wanted to carry on singing, so I let them sing with me.

Spontaneity in children is something quite special. People from the south suffer from pride and embarrassment and are too bothered about making a *'male figura'*, which means to show themselves up whereas a *'bella figura'* means you have impressed everybody. This is instilled in their minds from childhood.

Hardly much work was done this morning because the children were going to have their Carnival Party. Forty five minutes into the lesson one of the children came in dressed up as Zoro. That was it. It was time to get into the party spirit and dress up. One mother arrived with home-made biscuits called *chiacchiere* which means 'to gossip'. The children dashed out to change into their carnival outfits and what a transformation! In came Scarlett O'Hara from *Gone with the Wind* in a beautifully made rich blue velvet dress. Then the Dame from Florence in a rich golden dress, then the Princess of Flowers and Serena was the Princess of the Horses, Sandrokan followed, it was Luca. Mario was dressed up as a little devil a red cloak round his shoulders and two horns on his head. The rest of the boys were dressed as punk rockers, displaying their purple coloured hair and scary looking masks. The caretaker brought in the recorder, the music started playing and the children started dancing, myself included. Then he began filming and the mothers and fathers started clapping and rocking their heads.

Carnival is a serious business in Italy. Every city, town and village just goes bonkers. Four consecutive evenings of dancing until around four in the morning. The local village halls turn into family social clubs. Big home-made giant *maccheronies* are cooked especially for the occasion, a rich tomato sauce cooked with pork and spices. Groups of people dress up and wear a mask so that you cannot recognise who they are. They go in and out of the dance halls and dance and make a show, telling jokes and generally having fun.

Like Cinderella I had to leave – it had just turned midday and I had to be in Messina for three. But I was now in a party mood and didn't want to go.

My next lesson was to be with adults, one of whom was a retired doctor of eighty. His motivation for learning English was so that he could go back to Scotland where he had had a serious head operation, to thank his surgeon and converse in English. Most of my teaching day was spent with either very young people or mature people.

My earliest memories of dressing up was dressing up for my First Holy Communion at St Osburg's School in Coventry. I was only seven years old and was deeply in love with Philip Thorne. He was my little hero but he never ever noticed me. You could say I was a pretty little Italian girl, and stood out from the others because of my dark brown 'cow' eyes and natural curly hair which fell prettily down my shoulders. I was the only little girl that had a long communion dress that went to the ground, all my other class mates had communion dresses that went to their knees. We all looked like little brides. My parents had my dress made and the night before the special occasion I had to have my hair done in ringlets by a neighbour. She lived in a tiny terrace house in Sandy Lane. The house was where the Climax entrance is now. Unfortunately the old terraces were knocked down to make way for progress, gradually taking away the legacy of old industrial Coventry. The front door opened straight into the front room. It was cosy with pretty matching curtains. The lady was Irish and there was certainly an Irish feel to the surroundings. My hair was twisted round cotton stripes and pinned together the whole night. The next morning I was dressed, pretty and ready. We were not allowed to have breakfast before Communion so we had a Communion breakfast in the big hall at the school after Mass. Philip Thorne was sitting opposite me, looking so handsome in his smart little grey suit, his red tie and short trousers. But alas, he did not notice me, even if I thought I had the prettiest communion dress. I had little white bows spaced out on the bodice and of course my pretty ringlets under my veil and I was even wearing white transparent gloves to match my little bag and my little prayer book. He was more intelligent than me in class as he could do his sums without the help of buttons to count. My mum was strict with me even from an early age. I could not even play kiss-chase to my heart's content because a little birdie would be watching me and would tell tales on me to my mum. I so much wanted Philip Thorne to catch me and kiss me, but oh no, it was always James. James was not as good-looking as Philip. He had reddish hair and was taller than Philip but I was put off by his knobbly knees. He was always nice to me but I really was not interested.

2nd March 2001

I got up feeling tired again. This time it was my fault. I had been staying up late most evenings to watch *The Costanzo Show*, the chat show on television which starts at about 10.30 p.m. and finishes at about 12.30 a.m. If they omitted the commercials it would last just over an hour. Just before the beginning of the show the pretty blonde presenter always says, 'Now it's time for the usual appointment with the Maurizio Costanzo Show', Show pronounced 'SSHOOOO'.

Dr Costanzo, as he is known, is three times smaller than Pavarotti. He has a television audience of about 6,000. The guests he invites to his show are from all walks of life, actors, comedians, politicians, surgeons, writers, film directors, the ordinary people and even tramps... They are invited to talk about different issues which could be reality or just a theme, for example, the homeless, success, love, psychology, friendship, beauty, travel, political issues, spiritualism, religion, rape, catastrophes etc. I personally think that he has more power than Berlusconi or Ciampi. He is Italy's sugar daddy. His guests are seated in a row, facing the audience in a small theatre in Rome. Behind the guests the musical band are called to play whenever there is a break or even to play along depending on the mood of the conversation. For example, if the theme is on love they might play a romantic tune like *Titanic* or *Love Story*, or if there is an embarrassing moment during a conversation between the guests the band is there to break the ice, or, if there is a heated discussion something lively is played to avoid any further antagonism. The conductor of the band is called Demo Morselli and is about 45, trying to look about 25 with long black hair and as he waves his stick his hair bounces all over the place. He is very casually dressed usually with his shirt buttons open so that he can show off his hairy chest and gold necklace round his neck. The blonde singer gets up to sing any song that is requested from rock to blues or even Napolitan folk songs to English pop. When there is an international guest the interpreter is invited too. When she interprets, you can hear her posh English accent and her posh Italian accent. She is very professional. Important personalities like Dr Bernard or even Rosemary Althea have frequently been invited. My favourite personality is Vittorio Sgarbi. He was the Under Secretary of the Minister for the Protection of Cultural Assets in Italy and knows everything on art and is also a strong art critic. Not only does he criticise art, he wouldn't think twice in punching his adversary in the face in front of the television camera. Whenever he appears he always causes a stir, he never minces his words. He deplores the way in which the art assets in Italy are not always conserved carefully. Another very interesting guest is Platinette, Italy's number one drag-queen. Her real name, rather, his real name is Mauro sometimes called Maurizio Coruzzi. When Platinette appears on television she is extravagantly dressed. She wears an almost white, very high wig, just like Mrs Simpson. She is obese, but that doesn't stop her from dressing up to be as sexy as she can make herself look. Before an appearance on any show on Italian television, she takes her time in making up her face. Her lipstick is usually a shocking red that goes perfectly with her manicured hands with red painted nails. Her eyelashes are false because they are black and very long. Her eyebrows are neatly shaped, brushed to perfection and plucked just at the right spot to make her look expressive. The eye liner meticulously painted round her sea-blue eyes, to make them look bigger and more beautiful. Eye shadow and rouge artistically applied. More woman than a normal woman I would say. Her clothes are no less spectacular. Sometimes she wears organza in deep blue with sequins down the side to give it the glamorous touch and her show of jewellery is just as flashy with her necklaces which lay over her very heavy chest. I think she/he ought to conduct her own talk show for I think Platinette is intelligent, witty, ironic and interesting. In an interview he stated that he obviously wasn't a woman and thinks like a man and makes decisions as a man would do. He added that he liked to think he is a man 'with balls'. The Italian expression *'con le palle'* means to be like a real man in every aspect. He liked to play and act just like one who uses a computer using all its options. He thought that people might say that he was a man but with his ovaries. It was better to have two lives than one. Maurizio is also a disc jockey on a radio show which is on air every morning. He discusses real life live on the show and when he talks to his listeners he is very sensitive to their opinions and adds his opinions which could never be considered condescending or arrogant.

The night before, a woman who professed that she could make contact with a UFO was on the show. She declared that she had been in a coma for days and when she had come out of her coma, she was able to converse with the unknown and that they were able to contact her by writing. That is, if she wanted to speak to them all she had to do was get a blank sheet of paper and she would start scribbling as if in cryptic code. Members of the audience were invited to ask her questions. There would be silence for a moment then her hands would start scribbling faster than a shorthand writer. She could tell people about their past, present and future and all this was demonstrated on the show.

Once Rosemary Althea was on the show and of course she was speaking to all the family loved ones who had passed away and were in the show spiritually. Dr Costanzo gives everybody an interview. He shifts from one guest to another by placing his stool next to the guest's chair. At his discretion he allows the guests to talk about their experience or book they may have written. And if ever something is said that he thinks might cause offence, he will cleverly steer the conversation. He loves to invite the personalities from the *Big Brother* show and if ever the discussion falls on sex and attraction, you can bet The Californian Dream Men come on to do their striptease act. Of course that's a very popular entertainment. As they prance to the music, the cameraman zooms and takes a close-up of the women guests and even the women in the audience, and you should see the expressions on their faces. 'It's about time too', I say.

Italian television has nothing but beautiful women, mostly successful and glamorous and it's too much. The actresses are all thin and attractive, the reporters are all thin and attractive, the show girls, dancers and models and even the politicians are slim and attractive. You just feel like an old freak. The competition is too great. So much emphasis is placed on having a good appearance and if you have cellulite on your bottom or legs you've had it. You have to go to a masseur, or buy special creams or you must absolutely buy a machine with many wires and gadgets that are attached to your body. The muscles are pushed about backwards and forward by electrical impulses, while you sit and relax. It's like watching a person with a nervous tick, not just one but many. The commercials show Mr Universe with the most repulsive muscles moving to and fro. Very soon people will be walking along the road twitching as well as talking into their mobile phones. What has society come to? The men must have their hairy chests and backs waxed. The message is strong and clear. If you want to get on in the world you have to look like a Barbie doll. So it is about time I say that the men start to feel inadequate as we ordinary women would like to feel NORMAL.

My drive up the mountains was nearly okay... As I drove past the bumpy track, past the brook, a man started shouting at me. '*Signora torni indietro, non si puo' passare.*' 'Turn back you can't go that way.' I managed to make a three-point turn then heard a bang. I got out of my car to check the tyres, they looked okay, got back into the car and drove back onto the road. If I had been less English, when I saw the diversion sign which hadn't yet been removed, I wouldn't have gone down the ditch! I did not think in the Sicilian way. I'm getting there though. You have to be one step ahead. I used to think that Sicilians were terribly cunning and devious, but it's just a question of survival. To them it's second nature, I'm still on rotation.

Italy or should I say Sicily is really useless when passing information to the public. However, in the south it doesn't make the slightest difference. It's all a formality. Jobs are got by recommendation. For example, if someone is about to retire from a job, she tells someone about it, it may be someone in the family, a relative, a neighbour or a friend. The job is already spoken for before one sends in an application.

Just then the school bus appeared behind me and Giovanni put his head out of the school bus window and bawled, '*MAESTRA D'INGLESE. CHEECHER, CHEECHER!*' All the kids started waving and shouting at me frantically. The yellow school bus was bobbing about even more until the driver roared like a lion at his passengers to sit still.

I got into the little school and got my usual welcoming kiss from the infants. Cettina decided to stay in the class, she shouted at the young kids in her Sergeant-Major voice, every time that happened the whole building made a hiccup and the children would jerk their shoulders up straight. Martina the quietest of them all was sitting in front of me. She too has big brown eyes with very soft mousy hair falling to her shoulders. Whenever I tried to get her to say something she would just whisper or may just start to cry. The other infants were already used to her constant crying and never took any notice of her. She wore her little blue apron, neatly ironed with its pretty white collar. At elementary school the children have to wear a sort of overall that is buttoned at the back to keep them tidy. The boys have to wear them too, except theirs are shorter. In the past the boys had to wear them in just the same way as the girls which made them look sissies. To help the children memorise the new words I had taught them, I drew little pictures on the board with the words to the side. I wrote as plainly as possible but Cettina got up to the board and instructed me to write *in corsivo*, that is, the letters joined together. When I was six I was taught to write with a pencil and to write letters without joining them together. Personally I think that the English idea makes more sense but I had to pretend to be grateful for her intervention. Then she went out of the room. Martina started crying again. All she did was cry and cry and cry and cry. We all wanted her to stop, it became annoying, irritating and unbearable. I wanted to grab her by her tiny feet, give her a twirl in the air, fling her through the windows and across the mountains to the fairies so that they could sort her out. But no, I couldn't do that. I sat her on my lap and patiently asked if her head was hurting, if her ears were hurting and finally when I asked if it was her tummy she just cried even louder and nodded her head. I suddenly announced that a little bit of magic was going to be performed and I needed the help of all the kids in the class. They had to shout the numbers up to ten while I rubbed her stomach in clockwork fashion to each count. On the tenth count we all had to throw her pain out of the window. 'One, two, tree, foor, faive, sex... and out it goes...' '*E' andata via?*' 'Has it gone?'

To every question there was a no with a nod of her head. So then we started counting again. It was only after a third attempt when the little kids managed to count to thirty that she eventually nodded yes and her sobbing stopped.

The pain suddenly seemed to materialise! It turned into a fuzzy cloud and lifted into the air. One of the children opened the window and out it went up and up and up to the sky, towards the mountains. It was the most natural thing that could have happened, the children didn't think it was anything extraordinary, as if they expected it to happen and, as the cloud lifted into the sky and disappeared, they started jumping up and down and clapping at the same time.

Cettina came back into the room to see what all the commotion was about but they all stopped clapping and sat down again and said nothing. I couldn't say anything at all as I was completely flabbergasted with my mouth slightly open and my eyes transfixed towards the window. I dared not explain the episode, she would have thought I was going out of my mind!

In the second class there was a little fat boy called Danilo. Danilo was Marina's brother and he tried hard to learn. He reminded me of Billy Bunter with his little dark glasses. Every time food was mentioned he started rubbing his little stomach with his hand and moved his little tongue from left to right. He once described how his father would slit a pig's throat open when it was time to slaughter it. His description was so vivid I think any city kid would have felt quite sick just by listening to it.

Having taught them the days of the week with simple phrases, such as, 'On Monday I go riding, on Tuesday I play tennis, on Wednesday I visit friends, etc.', I then went on to ask each one of them, 'What do you do on… Monday?' Each child had to give me one of the answers. When it was time to go Danilo would collect my bric-a-brac together, close the zip of my Mary Poppins bag, get my register and carry everything to the car.

I passed a man on his donkey, with sacks laid on both sides of the donkey's back and a lady, who may have been in her early sixties. Over her head she had a sort of rag cloth rolled like a hard doughnut and on top of that she was balancing two sacks on her head. Her hip movements were interesting to watch, from right to left and left to right like the movements of the back of the donkey that was just a few paces in front of her. Maybe that's where the fashion models get their ideas from.

It was a quarter to nine when I came out of my lesson at the language school. I walked wearily to my car parked a few streets back from the school. What should I see but a flat tyre!

9th March 2001

I was feeling anxious at the thought of having another punctured tyre. I was lucky that my tyre had gone flat in the city, it now entered my mind that this could happen again in the mountains.

It was really downcast this morning and surreal as I saw the clouds in patches around me and even below me as I drove along the mountains. My perplexity soon vanished when I saw the little children waiting for me, making the long drive up worthwhile. They were excited this morning because I was going to give them their English text books called *Popcorn*: *Popcorn* was a big coloured text book with words and pictures very attractively laid out with an easy activity book to go with it, a bit like the English drawing books you can buy in the paper-shops. They were very keen to write their name, class and even the teacher's name in the front cover in the spaces provided. Charlie the rabbit on his colourful scooter was the character of the book with his friend called Molly the Tortoise. They had already learnt to say, 'My name is...', but then they heard Charlie introduce himself on the tape and say, 'Hello, my name is Charlie. I'm Charlie the Rabbit. What's your name?' Charlie's voice was quite comical as its intonation went up and down and was long and drawn out. Charlie introduced all his friends who were in the book in the park including Molly the Tortoise, and every time they said hello the little kiddies said hello back. Then Charlie decided to sing the rainbow song. That was great too because the kids had also learnt to say the colours in English. Cry-baby was ready to cry again. Oh no, I thought, not again. The children's eyes looked cross and stared hard at her, willing her to stop, which she did to my relief. 'Red and yellow and pink and green, orange and purple and blue I can sing a rainbooooooooooooooo' what next, I saw a big blob of blood spill onto Giovanni's new *Popcorn* book. Blop, blop, blop, blop. Giovanni quite calmly tilted his head backwards and just got up to walk towards the tiny bathroom. I ran after him into the bathroom. Poor Giovanni, big drops of blood just dripped out of his nostrils. I grabbed hold of the paper towels, wetted them with the cold water from the running tap and put them round the back of his neck and held his head upwards. The caretaker came in and then Cettina. Giovanni was very mature about his little problem and kept as calm as possible, he didn't panic or cry. I didn't panic either strangely enough. Sabrina, the other teacher, who was always jolly and friendly, looked at me and laughed. 'Something always happens when you're around.' 'Never a dull moment!' I answered in Italian and indeed there never was.

Giovanni soon came back into the class with a relieved smile showing off his gap in his mouth where his tooth was missing. His face seemed to take on the expression like the Joker from *Batman and Robin*. His cheeks folded widely, as if to say, 'Nothing can scare me anymore from now on!' Serena had by then come to me and put her arm round my neck. I was gradually falling in love with them.

The second class 'la seconda' were also working on their new books too. *Stepping Stones 3*. Luca wasn't at all enthusiastic when he discovered that he had to connect letters to symbols, then he read the instructions, and decided it was like playing a game. The rest of the morning went quite quickly and smoothly and I was well satisfied with my morning lessons. Then Danilo helped me take all my paraphernalia to the car. I reversed back into a semicircle ready to set off on my track down the mountains.

I got stuck in a 'goat' jam. A farmer on his donkey leading about six goats with bells round their necks just trotted along. The farmer was carrying an umbrella under his arm, maybe to ward off the evil spirits or to protect himself from the sun or the rain. Chickens and dogs got in the way as I drove down the track into the misty and mysterious mountains.

As I drove along the beaten track I thought about the strange names of the villages and the derivation of the names of the villages.

In Greek mythology the Greek gods often left their home on Mount Olympus, the highest mountain in Greece and travelled all over the world and of course Dionysus and Efesto took a liking to Sicily.

Over the other side of the valley there is another dry river, and the village in the valley is called *Fiumedinisi*. '*Fiume*' means river '*di*' means 'from' and '*Nisi*' comes from the Greek name 'Nisa'. Because of its name it has been hypothesised that *Fiumedinisi* was founded by the Chalcidians. (The Greeks, Chalcidians from Euboea established their first colony in Sicily round 735 BC). To the Greeks this also meant woods and cities sacred to Dionysus. Dionysus was the god of wine, vegetation and of ecstasy. The Latin word for Dionysus is 'Bacco'. He was the son of Giove and Semele, and was educated and brought up by the mythological nymphs called 'Nisiadi or sometimes called Naiadi'. The Greek gods resided on Mount Olympus. Dionysus was almost as important as Zeus. He was often venerated and there were many feasts dedicated to him.

In Greek and Roman mythology they were spiritual beings which personified the force of nature, lived in the mountains, in the caves, and in the groves, in the woods, near the brooks, rivers and seas. They were beautiful beings having a passion for music and dance, they were not exactly mortals but lived very long lives. Their cult was strictly connected to Pan, their lover, their guide and companion. Pan was the son of Ermes and lived in the mountains and caves. He was half man and half animal and had horns, goat calves and hooves. He was gifted with inexhaustible sexual vigour and always had his way with the unfortunate fairies who got in his way.

One version of the legend says that he punished one fairy. She did not want to give in to his passions and tried to escape her destiny. He chased after her and punished her by changing her into waterfall canes. Then he took a piece of the waterfall cane and transformed it into a sort of a flute called '*siringa*'. From that day on he played his *siringa* to produce a certain kind of melody which he played while the fairies danced. It is said that the melodies could be heard in the depths of the woods at night which was an indication that he was wandering around the woods. I guess the word 'CURNUTO' ('*CORNUTO*' in Italian) derives from this story. In Italy if a man is CORNUTO, it means that his wife has been unfaithful. *Corno* means horn, thus a man has been horned. There was even racial division between the nymphs – the Draids were the wood and tree nymphs, the Nereidi were the sea nymphs (Nereidis were the children of Nereo and Danilo and they lived at the bottom of the sea and numbered between fifty and one hundred. They loved to play with the fish and play in the waves of the sea). The Naiadis were the waterfall, brooks, and river nymphs. (Naiadi were the children of Zeus and had the power to heal. They were worshipped by the sick and infirm, who drank from the water springs of the mountains.)

And while all this was going on, Efesto or Vulcan, the God of Fire, worked on as a blacksmith in his forge at the bottom of the mystical volcano of Etna. Efesto was the son of Zeus and the Goddess Era. Efesto was very ugly and was born lame. Because of his ugly appearance he was banished from Olympus. Efesto did not despair, he went back to Olympus and married Aphrodite, Goddess of Love. Then they came to Sicily to settle down and you might say make a living. He was a dedicated blacksmith. His job was to make armours and jewellery for the other gods and goddesses. He was not the only Cyclop to inhabit the island round the volcano of Etna. Other Cyclopes, including the one-eyed cannibal giant, Polifermo, lived there too.

Mount Etna is the largest active volcano in Europe. No wonder the Cyclopes decided to settle in Sicily, it was because of the rich volcanic soil round Etna. The lower slopes bear a lush crop of citrus fruits, oranges, tangerines and lemons, as well as figs, almonds, grapes and olives. The terrain near the summit is barren and there is little else but ash and hardened lava. There are small craters from which hot gases and lava sometimes burst forth, and of course when that happens, it is because Efesto is busy working.

Empedocles, the philosopher (492–432 BC), was said to have leaped into the crater to his death to ensure immortality. He wanted the citizens of that time to believe that he was called in by the gods. I am sure that when he got to the bottom of the crater he found a great surprise – probably Efesto making some beautiful jewel for his wife or maybe having a chat with the one-eyed giant while having a break. Whatever activity they may be up to, to this day they can be heard.

Empedocles' philosophy was that there were four major elements, earth, air, fire and water. A great discovery maybe in his time. But interesting when he says there are two opposite forces – love and hate, friendship and discord.

<u>13th March 2001</u>

Oh, what a beautiful day. It was glorious. My daffodils had sprung up, I had bought back the bulbs from England.

As I got nearer to the school I could see Carmelita come out of a cobbled lane and then Daniel out of another cobbled lane, looking very serious. Erimi is an austere little village perched on the summit of the hill, a mysterious magic place where no one ever goes, except for its inhabitants and the children at the school. It's a very steep drive up cobbled stones, then left into a sort of alleyway, then right again up another very steep cobbled lane where the road twists and turns up the side of the mountain, sufficient space for one car, then a big swerve into a sort of platform square, then left again onto an even steeper hill until you reach the top to park the car next to the entrance of the school. At every turning I had to stop the car and put it into first gear. Then you park the car outside the school which looks more like a tower with its small courtyard overlooking the green mountains and over the roofs and balconies of the scattered houses below.

Giovanni was as right as rain, his nose back to normal. He showed me his homework and wanted to know if he had missed anything important after he had to leave the lesson because of his nosebleed. I'm not good at drawing, my sketches are comical and crooked but I managed to draw Erimi on a mountain with a rainbow in the background and Charlie the Rabbit sitting in the courtyard. I coloured the rainbow and wrote the name of the colours along the rainbow. They copied my masterpiece, writing the words in English then I gave them all flash cards with the name of the colours written in English. They had to recognise the colour and match it to the words, which were then to be coloured in. We sang the rainbow song and went out into the courtyard to play hopscotch. I had got the caretaker to draw squares with a chalk on the ground. Then I got a pebble and dropped it onto the square, which had numbers written on them. In turn they threw the little stone and hopped and jumped until they reached the pebble. Then we played the word and letter game. I gave six children flash cards with the figure of the number and six with the words of the number and separated them into two lines. Every time I called out a number they had to meet at the centre i.e. the child with the letter flash card had to step forward and meet with the child with the same number but written in figures. I got them to exchange their cards and to repeat 'thank you'. Then we played *The farmer's in his den*. There is nothing like playing with the kids in Erimi. You can pretend to be one of them and realise that true living is playing in the fresh air and having fun in such an enchanting place. Our voices echoed into the mountains and we could shout and scream as much as we wanted. It was our music of life. Of course our nymph friends were playing *The farmer's in his den* too, except that every time they skipped they skipped about four metres above the ground into the air just as fairies do.

The second class saw a video of how English oral exams were performed. The children were pleased to see that they were able to understand and respond to the questions that were asked by the examiner in the film. I then sat them in a semicircle round me and questioned them one by one more or less in the same way. If one of the children could not respond immediately, the others who knew the answer were impatient to answer for him. Marina suddenly pulled off one of her buttons from her apron to give to me because I did not have a button in my Mary Poppins bag. Then, when I was ready to go, a little squabble would start amongst them about who was to carry what for me, and who was to accompany me to the car.

As I drove home I considered how different it was teaching in Erimi and teaching in my language school in Messina. The children from Erimi came from hardworking families. Most of them work as foresters or manage their own farms. Because of little contact with the rest of the world their old dialect, mannerisms and ideas are kept alive. One or two of the children have computers, nevertheless the influence of their grandparents and the simplicity of their parents' lifestyle did reflect on them. The children I taught in the city paid to have English lessons and they not only had English lessons as extra scholastic activity, they also went horse riding, or played tennis, or went swimming, and every child in the class possessed a computer. They owned their own mopeds too, as well as having two holidays a year.

16th March 2001

I got as far as Sirio, one of the villages I have to pass, and in the square a sign said there were road works ahead and the main bypass was closed off. I parked the car in the square and went into the bar, the same bar at which I had had coffee when the headmistress had brought me over the very first day. The lady recognised me immediately and before I could open my mouth she opened the door behind her and called out to her daughter to come down and meet me. I politely put on an interested face. I was made to feel like a sort of celebrity so I tried to be as nice as pie, even though deep down I really wasn't at all interested. I had to listen to the daughter as she went on about her studies and what she wanted to do in life and how important it was to know how to speak English. All I wanted to ask was which other way could I go if not through the main road! An elderly gentleman with a weather-beaten face and looking very fit happened to be in the bar at the same time and suggested that I follow him. I politely cut short my conversation and left, grateful that the man had come to my rescue. As I turned the last bend before reaching Erimi I saw Adriano wave to me enthusiastically as he was waiting for the school bus to pass. He had beautiful blue eyes just like the guy in the chewing gum with baking soda commercial. A really happy-go-lucky temperament with a strong willingness to learn.

Mario was back today and I thought that would be it. I was expecting a difficult time ahead but to my delight Mario sat right next to me and started talking to me in dialect. He wanted to tell me something that was important to him and because of his speech impediment, I found it very difficult to understand, what he was trying to tell me. While all this was going on, Giovanni was jumping up and down opening and closing his book, spoiling Mario's determined concentration in trying to talk to me. Frustrated at not being able to get over what he wanted to say to me Mario suddenly went towards Giovanni, got his book and slammed it down hard on the desk in front of him. I sensed that

Mario wanted to show his intention of wanting to learn, understand and communicate and I guess the reason for his bad behaviour most of the time, was just his frustration at not being able to communicate, and most of all, at not being understood. It might have been the beginning of another class fight but just then Sabrina gently knocked on the door to announce that the photographer had arrived. As it happened all the children were present that day so we had a group photo taken in the courtyard. It was a welcome interruption for the children. The photographer was an elderly man, probably already a retired gentleman. He didn't have much agility in his movements so it was us the teachers who were trying to put them together. I was invited to stand amongst them with my hair blowing out of place. I told them all to repeat 'cheese', but as always, as the photographer clicked, someone closed his eyes. The photographer just wanted to get on with it.

Little time was left after so much time had been spent in lining the children up for their individual photo although not all of them had their photos taken because not all of the mothers could afford to pay for the extra photo. In class 2 Danilo was bullying Tommaso. Everybody bullied Tommaso, he was everyone's scapegoat and I found this intolerable and every time it happened I went straight to his defence and did my best to make them feel guilty. I handed out copies of a clown that had an extraordinary body. I wanted to teach the verb 'to have' as well as parts of the body. So I started by saying I have two eyes, one nose etc. etc. Each tried to remember as I got them to repeat one by one. Then I wrote the parts of the body on the board and they had to write the words on the body of the picture of the clown. Then I taught them that the clown HAS. I wrote a couple of simple sentences on the board so that it was clear to them the difference in the use of I have, and he has. When we had finished this exercise, I took out an old magazine which had the pictures of the Royal Family in it. We cut out the pictures and did a family wall chart. There was also a big picture of the Queen and the Trooping of the Colours. I got Alessio to copy out a simple paragraph describing what Trooping of the Colours was and before I knew it, it was time for me to go. Marina gave me some more buttons she had collected especially. She remembered the tape, in which the buttons were used to illustrate prepositions, e.g. the white button is near the big red button, etc. etc. I now felt part of the school, and the more I got to know the children the more I got to like them. It was certainly well worth the drive and the distance to the school. It was not an ordinary place, or school. It was time for me to leave again.

I drove slowly round the last awkward bend of the mountain. I had to stop the car suddenly! There was a herd of goats trotting towards me... Millions of them. I couldn't believe what I was seeing, some clip out of the film, *The Ten Commandments* maybe – or maybe the nymphs were playing a joke on me. Billy goats and nanny goats with bells under their necks jingling, tinkling away, as if all the goat species suddenly appeared before me. It was an enormous tintinnabulation of bells echoing through the mountains. It was me and the goats. I could imagine the bird's-eye view from above. My little black Ford Fiesta immobile while the goats surrounded my car, I was like a little black flattened tarantula completely sedated stuck in the middle of nowhere. 'You can't possibly be frightened of goats!' I told myself as I wind up my car door windows. All I could do was gape at their horns as they trotted by. Some had long horns, some very long horns, and many of them had long and twisted horns like the shape of an elongated wire spring. I must have waited for about five minutes, but the time seemed interminable as my eyes were fixed on their horns all pointing to the direction I was coming from with their shepherd behind them. I was trapped. My mind went to Pan from Greek mythology. I could just see him now with the long spiral horns on his head, intimidating and wild. The five long minutes eventually passed by and I slowly got my breath back. The fairies were hiding behind the bushes watching me. Whether I was being observed because of the comical situation I had got myself in or maybe they were there to give me moral support. After all they were only goats!

19th March 2001

I had hoped I would find no more surprises in making my way up to the school. No such luck. As we got as far as Sirio, (I was racing behind Cettina and Grace who were both driving in the car in front of me), we found the main bypass was completely closed. We had to drive up a very steep narrow alleyway at an angle of about 80° and veer the car right. The alleyway was not meant for cars. It was the sort of district where I guess most of the inhabitants lived, houses squashed together on both sides of the pathway which was no wider than a corridor. If I had wanted to get out of the car I could not, there was no space to open the door. Not only that, the road went suddenly down and then suddenly up again and if you were lucky enough to drive on without any oncoming traffic it was an achievement. I wondered what it was like to live in a place like this. I guessed there might be just old people but then I saw a young woman ushering her two children into her Suzuki to take them to school. There was another statue of the Black Madonna fitted into the wall, at the part of the path which was the widest, then following another bump, right turn down the steep cobbled lane with my feet firmly pressing against the brake pedal and the clutch pedal, back to the main road. One slight distraction, or if the lane was icy and one could go flying past the main road into the valley itself. I could just see myself sitting in the car doing a balancing act at the edge of the road waiting for some superman to come and rescue me. He would graciously carry me up into the sky and then gently lay me down on a safe rock, give me a romantic kiss and flitter away... or even Pan, but out of the two I should prefer Superman, Pan would find it quite difficult to carry me, especially with his having to carry the weight of his horns too. Then, oh yes, I had to drive down the brook and stony path. If my car had a soul it would have wondered why I was putting it through so much punishment. The morning was going to continue as it had started.

When I arrived at the school I could sense there was

something wrong. The children were not as boisterous as they usually were and there was this feeling of 'the quiet before the storm'. There had been a lot of disquiet before I arrived and the mood now was definitely pungent. The atmosphere was electric. Whether it was due to the place, one's senses became highly attuned to the changes in the feel of the ambience and frame of mind of the people around you. I could almost touch it.

Little Mario was restrained and despondent and somehow it affected the general disposition of the other children. I got on with my lesson as I had planned. Charlie the Rabbit and his friends were in his farm and he was describing the animals with a simple nursery rhyme… 'Moo, moo says the cow, Quack, quack says the duck, meow, meow says the cat…' and so on and so on. The children had their colourful books open looking at the picture of the farm with Charlie the Rabbit in the middle of it all. Mario just sat in his little chair with his arms folded in front of him and his book closed with an expression of anger, hate and revenge in his beautiful little blue eyes. Soon the children started to tell me what had happened. Mario had been severely reprimanded by the other teachers because he had pulled down an old poster from the wall. It happened before I arrived. The teachers hadn't asked him why he had done it. My guess was that there was little space for any more posters to be put up. My poster of the family with English names was still lying flat on the spare desk. The caretaker hadn't got round to rearranging the posters to include the English one.

As the saying goes, it was one of those days! The children in second class were just as agitated as the children from the first class. The harsh reality that some of these children do come from difficult circumstances suddenly became apparent. I detest bullying and victimisation. Tommaso was the only boy who hadn't wanted his English book – (not him but his father. Parents have to pay for their children's books in Italy) – I thought I could solve the problem. The moment I said that I could lend him mine until I could get hold of another copy, one of the children made a harsh comment which I thought was shocking, coming from such a young mind. 'Typical, he gets the teacher to get him a free copy. It's not right, his father's got the money!' Perhaps Tommaso's parents couldn't understand the importance of education and that education could determine a child's future. His parents appeared to belong to another era when education was meant only for the rich.

Sicily is divided into two social classes, the ordinary people doing ordinary jobs and the high class society of a high cultural level and financial stability. The high-class society can be seen mixing together in the libraries and museums where there is an exhibition of paintings or viewing a collection of antique furniture which may be on sale. The women beautifully dressed, whatever their age, with beautifully painted finger and toe nails and flashing their make-up and jewellery and the latest fashion in bags and sandals. Some of the people of the village might have had minimal schooling themselves and although they were not very old, their way of thinking belonged to a generation that only belonged to the poor peasants at the beginning of the century, maybe because they were born and bred in the same village and their world was confined in their little paradise. Tommaso was the youngest and the smallest in the class but he had a very quick mind and wanted to justify his situation to the others. Marina happened to be absent this morning and the aggressiveness of the boys seemed even stronger. Tommaso's life was not as carefree and childish as it should be. Whatever explanation he tried to give to his classmates didn't make any difference. He wanted to cry and was fighting back his tears. 'Don't start,' shouted one of the boys, as if their provocation had not been cruel enough to provoke his outcry. Might these children grow into suspicious, hard adults, just as the rugged surroundings they were growing up in? It wouldn't surprise me if these children would grow into suspicious hard people, as adults, just as the rugged surroundings they were growing up in.

I ended up giving a morality lesson, let's say a bit like the religious education (RE) lessons I used to have every morning in my secondary school, Bishop Ullathorne.

St Luke's Gospel and that of St Mathew was hammered into our heads at Bishop Ullathorne School. After morning assembly, when we had to pray and sing hymns, we had to have our first hour of religious education with our class teachers and sometimes we received instructions from the Catholic priest too. Class discussion used to take place about life in general, it was a pre-life training of how one should be a good Catholic. Personally I think there was too much emphasis on religion. We used to have Mass in class on Fridays and I was probably the only one who did not have Holy Communion. We had to go to confession every three weeks, if we wanted to receive Holy Communion. My sins were always the same so at a certain point I stopped going to Confession.

May is the month of Mary, Our Lady. We were encouraged to say the Rosary during our lunch hour. Bishop Ullathorne, Secondary School was an all girls school then. Every afternoon after lunch there we knelt on the hard marble floor outside the Headmistress' Office repeating the Hail Mary after the teachers. I hung about with four other girls, Mary, Linda, Carol and Anne. We wanted to be good little Catholic girls. One afternoon in the month of May we were kneeling down with rosary beads in our hands trying to be as reverend as possible. I started to hiccup. 'Hail Mary, hic hic, full of grace, hic hic, the Lord, hic, is, hic, with… thee, hic hic…' My friends started giggling quietly with their heads bent down looking pious and religious. My embarrassment got worse as my hiccups got louder and louder, interrupting the holiness of the moment. My four friends' heads and shoulders started to jig up and down without any restraint. It became painful not to giggle, and the more we tried to be serious the more we burst into fits of giggles. A fit of prolonged and uncontrollable giggling followed. The five of us were suddenly marched out into the playground and told to contemplate on our misbehaviour and ask God for his forgiveness. My main sin was to disobey my parents. And with every good intention of not disobeying them again, the next time round, I just did.

My father being a Sicilian was very strict and so was my mother. Fourteen was a dangerous age and I was to be protected. When sex education was introduced, I was the only girl in the class who dared put up her hand when the question was asked, 'Who doesn't know about the facts of life?' The discussion was brought up amongst ourselves quite frequently and it was one morning, walking to school down Wainbury Avenue, that it was explained to me by one of my class mates, Frances. I just couldn't believe it when she went into details and to think that my mother and father had done or did these things! It was the third year and Miss Stynchcombe was our form teacher. She was tall and attractive, in her early thirties and had short blonde hair. She tried to explain to us the mystery of life, the difference between right and wrong and good and bad. I can still remember her name because she was one of the nicest teachers at the time. We all had a 'crush' on her. Miss Stynchcombe looked at me as if I was a little moron and I wanted to squash my head into my shoulders when the other members of the class turned to look at me too. Miss Stynchcombe proceeded to explain the facts by making simple drawings on the board. First she reminded us of our biology lessons about pollination then went to the point. So Frances Sutherland was right after all, I thought to myself.

The moment my parents discovered that I had learnt how children were born, they became stricter with me. My freedom was much more limited than that of my friends. They could have Saturday jobs, I couldn't, they could go on the school trip, I couldn't, they could meet on Saturdays and go shopping together, I couldn't. The only concession I had was that I could go to my friend's birthday party and I could invite my friends to my home, which I rarely did.

Mary was and still is my best friend. My very first day at Bishop Ullathorne School had been nerve racking. The chair next to mine was still empty and I hardly knew anyone in the class. Mary came up to me and asked, 'Is there anyone sitting in this chair?' She had thick mousy hair and was about my height, I was slightly taller. Her parents were Irish and mine were Sicilian. From that time on we stuck together. There were actually five of us who stuck together, but Mary and I understood each other well. Linda, Carol and Ann, Mary and myself were always together at playtime. Ann had blond hair and blue eyes, Carol had red hair and blue eyes, and Linda was the tallest and had chestnut hair and beautiful blue eyes. It was 1968 and we were in the third year in the third grade i.e. 3B and corporal punishment was legal. First and second grades were intelligent enough to take their O level or CSEs the third and fourth were not. Miss Stynchcombe was our form teacher. That year we were labelled as the bad class, a sort of year for regression a bit like the film *To Sir with Love*, we were not very popular with the teachers that year. Children who came out of the third and fourth grades were not expected to get jobs beyond hairdressing, or shop assistants, or working in some sort of box factory. The system then was quite complicated. We had two class exams a year, one before Christmas and the other before the summer holidays. All the calculations of test results of each academic subject were added together and depending on what we got out of 100 we were given our class places as our major achievement. If you came first or second in the summer exams you were moved up to the next grade. I had really missed the boat that year I was top of the class at Christmas and came third in the summer. My future was marked out and qualifications of any real value were to be got later at technical college. Classes A and B could study French and shorthand and consider university. I have to admit I was a lazy scholar, I could not get any help from my parents at home. Most of the children were of working-class families. I was the odd penny. I was the only girl who wore earrings. But we were happy and carefree. We used to lie on the grass sucking our ice lollies which were either long or in a triangular shape, it was the daydreaming years when there wasn't a care in the world. We would form a sort of pattern on the grass by resting our heads on each others back or thighs. Winter used to be winter with snow flakes falling softly and beautifully covering the open countryside beyond the school playgrounds and sports grounds. We would play in the snow, throwing big snow balls at each other and creating ice patches where we took it in turn to slide as far as we could go, ruining our shoes and getting filthy black from the sludge. One afternoon the winter of that year, the snow started to fall and continued right into the afternoon. It must have snowed for three hours non-stop. The traffic was at a standstill and by half past three the roads were impassable. It was fantastic. All seven thousand pupils, including the boys from the grammar and secondary school had to walk. It was delightful, we all walked along Kenilworth Road all the way to the centre of Coventry. It continued to snow quite heavily on our walk home but we loved it. By the time I had got to 189

Barkers Butts Lane from Bishop Ullathorne School my strands of hair had turned into drops of ice and my face was as pink as a strawberry.

We had a very interesting timetable. We had cookery lessons, craft lessons, sewing lessons, RE, history, geography, chemistry and games and even dancing and drama. We used to walk from school to the centre of Coventry through the Memorial Park. We were not supposed to. My father never found out. There was a kind of regimental order in those days and having to wear a uniform made us feel like part of a military order with no sign of femininity. If we were caught not wearing our hats or berets we would get the strap the next day from the headmistress, Mrs Healy. How? Well, it was a Gestapo situation. The school prefects were given orders to note down in their little notebooks anyone not wearing a hat or beret or even pushing in at the bus stop. But as soon as we got out of sight we used to take off our school berets and throw them into the air, roll up our dull grey skirts at the waist so that you could see our knees, loosen our ties and laugh and joke and giggle and eat ice cream. We couldn't care less, we just enjoyed the freedom we had created for ourselves and time belonged to us. Once, while on one of our school journeys home on the bus we were all carrying our apple pies that we had made in our cookery lesson. My very first apple pie, of which I was so proud. The bus suddenly jerked and my beautiful apple pie landed on the passenger aisle of the red double-decker bus. The conductress, whose face looked like the face of a shop dummy – her skin was so powdered and she was wearing the ugliest lipstick, made me pick up my dismantled apple pie and throw it out of the bus. A kind of Mr Bean situation. Mary, who was sitting next to the window and next to me, just laughed and laughed and laughed until it was time for her to get off the bus. I had to laugh too and what remained of my apple pie was appreciated at home so I started making apple pies and apple crumbles every weekend. Sometimes Linda and I would buy some fresh strawberries and sit in the tiny park outside what used to be the Coventry Theatre which then became the Bingo Hall. The Coventry Theatre was grand and beautiful and it felt like a theatre, what a big big shame it got transformed into the Bingo Hall.

Every time we came out of the park gate my heart would miss a beat in case my father might be driving by and discover I was not safely on the bus. We used to talk about boys and our favourite TV programmes and how our lives would proceed and even death itself. School in those days was a preparation for life. We were in the third grade, which meant we could not do CSE or O levels. This did not bother us until the fourth year, but we proved the authorities wrong. After much debate we were the very first pupils of the third grade to do CSEs. It was a victory.

After giving the Erimi kids a morality lesson, there was little time left for English so we went out to play *What's the time, Mr Wolf?* Tommaso would not join in. One asks oneself who does the most damage to a child's happy upbringing, the parents or the school?

23rd March 2001

The weather forecast said it was going to be a warm day around 20° Celsius, but cloudy. The BBC weather forecast said there would be misty, ground frost and black ice in England. The sea was pale blue and calm and the blossom trees looked very pink – a kind of celestial celebration. In my garden, my daffodils were still in flower and my passion flowers were already opening. It was very hot sitting in the car, it's like sitting in a greenhouse, and if you can't find a parking space in the shade, when you open the car door, it's like going into a hot oven to be baked alive. The thought of driving through the tiny path again in Sirio was not a comforting thought, however, I was grateful that it was a clear day. I was now getting used to all the diversions and was becoming a good rally driver. It's something I've always wanted to do. I could imagine myself wearing a helmet and driving up and down the muddy roads in the alps of Switzerland in a rally competition. And after surviving the weather conditions and the obstacles and the possibility of winning, what a feeling of euphoria. My driving companion would be like me, a little crazy, perhaps a little wild too.

When I finally got to the school the children were still eating their big *paninos*. They were reluctant to go into the little cramped classrooms. Cristofaro and Mario were like two jack-in-the-boxes and like leaders of the gang, they were capable of influencing the rest of the children. We repeated the rainbow song, the kids didn't just sing they moved their little bodies to and fro to the beat of the music like the dwarfs from Snow White and the Seven Dwarfs. There happened to be an empty cardboard box in the cloakroom and one the children asked if we could make a house out of it. The caretaker wasn't doing anything so I asked him if he could make the box into the shape of a house. An hour later he walked into the class with a beautiful replica of a house, but without any windows and doors. We got to work and added the windows and doors and the curtains and even put up a picture of a family, cut out from a magazine. The girls drew pretty flowers round the wall. When we had finished, I printed the names of the parts of the house. I got them to draw their house and copy the words in English, roof, window, door, etc. We were all so proud of our little English house, it was the nicest doll's house the children had ever seen.

In my second class the children made a circle round me. I got out all my buttons and an empty jar and a pencil and placed them in the various position – in, on, under, above, near, between etc. and asked, 'Where is the small white button?' 'Under the jar', or 'next to the pencil' or 'between the jar and the pencil' was the answer, so on and so on. I questioned each child while the others stood around us. They jumped with excitement lifting their arms up with their fists closed when they got the answer right, or they would press their lips together with frustration when they got it wrong. There was always a little pushing and shoving between them, and as usual little Tommaso always got squashed out. I just picked his little body up and sat him on the desk right near me as I was determined that their apathy and intolerance towards him must stop.

On my way down the cobbled path, directly under the school, an old lady with bright red cheeks and big vivacious brown eyes stood outside her door. I stopped for a little chat about Erimi. She said there was a lot of peace and tranquillity, and most of the food she ate was home-made and home-grown. She led a very simple life. I reflected on what she had said and thought maybe with so much high technology and progress we were missing the point – maybe these people had found the true meaning of life itself. It was like talking to a simple country lady belonging to the seventeenth century.

That period could be compared to the industrial revolution in England when at first simple country folks worked at home sitting at their looms transforming silk and linen reels to cloth, then they went to the cities to work in the factories.

Around the 1400s, it was the beginning of the growth in the art of making silk. This was probably the most prosperous period for Sicily. Apart from the grain fields the main agricultural economy came from the planting of Mulberry groves. By the

1700s Mulberry groves covered about 11,869 hectares and the cultivation of mulberry and the breeding of silkworms became a flourishing industry in this area of Sicily. There was money to be made from this industry. The climatic conditions were favourable to this kind of cultivation. In 1842 there was a textile factory. It was called '*Fabbrica*' (Factory) by the locals. It specialised in the production of white, coloured and floral muslin, i.e. fine cloth used for dresses and also very fine table cloths of the highest quality. The factory was run by English and French experts employing 1,018 workers of whom 574 were women, 100 operators and 334 boys. 500 looms were worked by hand and there were also the new mechanically operated looms. Not only did people work in the factory, they also worked in the cultivation of silkworms. In that period obviously there was much less sophistication compared to the silk factories now, most of which are found in China. The factory produced 30,000 pieces of material which was exported to England, Holland, Finland and Turkey. What seemed to be a flourishing industry, providing work and security to 30 per cent of the local inhabitants, sadly in the end became a total failure. What might have developed into a colossal industry today unfortunately ended abruptly in 1855 when there were only 20 men, 16 women and 10 boys working in the factory. The death of this industry was caused by a new law – a high tax duty was introduced in 1850 by the King from Caserta (Caserta near Naples). In the same year the factory was completely destroyed by a tremendous flood. The French and English experts then set up another factory in Calabria in Favazzina. My guess is that they probably got exasperated trying to set up the plant again because of bureaucratic problems. Nothing has changed much since then. Young people are put off starting any plausible activity because of the bureaucratic problems. I think it is such a sad state of affairs. The best brains of Sicily are not in Sicily. They have to move away so that they can move forward in life as they know that whatever effort they put into looking for a prosperous future in Sicily it would be futile. There are some successful stories, however. Young graduates create their own cooperatives financed by the government – but before they are able to reach their goals they have to have their projects approved by the Region and if they know some political person who can help them they may eventually reach their objectives.

I brought up the subject about the production of silk in this area with my university students. It was quite evident that bureaucracy, fear of corruption, very little incentive and interest from the Government and local Government, have made the people what they are today. They are apathetic and resigned to accepting that there will be very little change or progress in the south. This present-day attitude is the result of centuries of suppression up to the time when Garibaldi landed in Marsala in 1860 and defeated the Bourbons. The unification of Italy came in 1870. There were poor relations between the north and the south of Italy and unfortunately Sicily became the backward colony of the rapidly industrialised north.

By 1900 there was a big exodus of Sicilians emigrating to other countries, primarily to America, then Australia and even in the 1950s to England and France, South America and of course to the north of Italy, mostly Milan and Turin.

I personally would like to see the Government introducing the industry all over again. Everything that does not work is blamed on the mentality of the people of the south and of course the Mafia which seems to be a very convenient reason. This only proves one point – that Sicily can never be part of Italy and that the Italian government does not want to, or even know how to, or even care to make an island with so many natural resources a rich industry for its people. It could be argued that Sicily is not capable of ruling itself. In 1946 Sicily was granted a certain amount of regional autonomy from Rome and the following year a Sicilian parliament was elected.

I believe that if there were to be outside interest, i.e. from China or from France and European investment the potential that can be got from the natural resources found on this island, could be bountiful. If the boot of Sicily were to be turned upside down, and Sicily were to be the industrious north, it would be providing not only the best industry for tourism, but also the best for the production of local wines and the exportation of exotic fruit such as kiwis, melons and lemons, the cultivation of sugar cane and sugar refineries, the olive groves and the production of olive oil and the manufacture of fine silk. The reality is that young Sicilians still have to leave their homeland to find work in the north and I suppose my little children from Erimi will have to go away if they want to make something of their lives in the future.

To make silk from silk worm it has to go through its various phases. It is said that to speed up the production of the silk from the worm the peasant women used to wrap the silkworm eggs in a piece of cloth and then placed it in their cleavage for incubation. This was done because the body temperature is 37 degrees, the same temperature needed for the incubation of the silk worm eggs. Maybe that's why Sicilian women have naturally big breasts. The process of transformation takes about 40 days from the time when the silk worm produces its eggs to the eventual production of silk thread. Then the threads have to be boiled and dried in a special way.

Savoca was one of the inland villages that prospered from the success in making silk. There is a legend in Savoca about the 'Miracle Veil' that goes back to the seventeenth century. A lady of the village was deep in debt and implored the Madonna to have a good harvest of silkworms so that she could pay back her debts. For this concession she promised to donate a veil made of silk, which was to be used as a cover for the Chalice which is used in Mass. The lady's prayers were answered as the harvest that year had been the best, never before that year had there been so many silkworms and so she was able to pay back all her debts. But the lady of Savoca forgot the promise she had made to the Madonna and did not donate any veil to the Church. The following year, as she was observing the silkworms, to her satisfaction she noticed that the silkworms were unusually big and so she presumed that the harvest would be even better than the year before.

She noticed that when the silkworms had finished making the thread, instead of closing themselves into their cocoons, the silkworms joined together as if breaking out into a sort of mutiny, and with their saliva made a thick tightly woven veil in the form of a square. Then all the woman's silkworms died, never to produce anything for her again. Disturbed by these events the lady abandoned the village of Savoca.

27th March 2001

It was a really beautiful summer's day, one of those rare days you sometimes get in May in England. The BBC forecast said there was black ice and fog in England while it was 25° Celsius here. Round the village of Erimi there are about 30 blossom trees, if not more. They were all in flower and it looked like a little Paradise, that is assuming that Paradise has a lot of blossom trees. The colours of the blossom tress, which I believe to be the laburnum tree, were of a vibrant ivory and a subtle yellow inside the petals, which looked like brilliant gold shining delicately. The rays of the sun caressed the gold within the petals and then bounced back into the air. The Woodland pixies had laboured day and night to make the trees the splendour and beauty of Erimi.

These fine creatures with their pointed ears and long thin arms and legs stay hidden from view to all but the most special of humans, particularly so to the innocent and pure. I could perceive a lot of energy and life around me as I drove into this little secret paradise. The fairies were singing merrily as they were cleaning out their habitats and the twittering and chattering of the birds was clear and sonorous. Three hours was a long time to spend with six-year-old children teaching English, but that was the case this morning. We put the miniature desks together to make a big table. I got cardboard paper used for making wall charts and laid three on the table and joined them together. Then I got one of the children and lay her on the chart and with a big crayon we traced her body onto the chart. Then the children helped me to draw the clothes over the body chart and then we put the names of parts of the body and clothes in English. I gave each child a task, one had to draw the nails and then write nails beside, then another the legs and knees, the skirt, collar, face, etc. etc. The first hour went by harmoniously as each child was intent on working on his patch of the body. The body took shape and character as I drew each part of the body as the children had wanted. Then we went out into the magic playground for a break. Teaching English to six-year-olds is a very difficult task, I would say a very big challenge. You have to be inventive and adapt to their ability and character so other skills have to be used. It isn't enough to have a good academic background, you have to be mother, psychiatrist, friend, teacher, a clown and a policewoman all in one. I used to feel intimidated when I first taught adults but I soon realised it was much more intimidating teaching young children and one other skill one learns is to be able to hide this feeling, so let's say you have to be a good actress too. This harmony was suddenly shattered by Mario, the little blue-eyed angel. The little angel suddenly turned into the little red devil. He had already hit Marina hard before going into class for the simple reason that he did not want to be disturbed. I had taken him to one side and said that he was to keep a promise and that he was going to be good. I got his little finger and my little finger and entwined them together and said we were about to make a very important pact and that he was going to make me an important promise. He nodded his head and I thought I had done the trick. I had not.

We had just returned into the class after playing *Ring a ring of roses* and *The farmer's in his den* when Mario turned suddenly towards Adriano and kicked him hard on the shins. Adriano yelled out aloud in pain and shock. I was horrified at the force of the kick. Adriano had not done anything to provoke Mario's bad behaviour. Adriano was one of the quietest and easiest children to teach. He was a model pupil and had a gentle face and manner. He had dark eyes and dark hair and had delicate lily-white skin. I was so shocked and angry that I went to Mario and wanted to shake him hard to liberate him of whichever evil spirit that might have been kindling in his angelic little body. '*Non hai mantenuto la promessa. Adesso non siamo piu amici!*' I said angrily. 'You have broken your promise and we are not friends any more!' The naughty fairies must have been in the vicinity trying to disrupt the harmonious magic and mood of the morning. The elf, with its tangled hair, getting together with the Nixes, the rejects of the fairy world, the Pucks, the bogeys and the hobgoblins, the evil fairies with their mischievous and evil spirits. Mario was their easy target.

By about 11 a.m. I should have already gone into my second

class, but my children were so engrossed with their exercises in their workbooks that I did not want to break the spell. So there I remained until midday while Charlie the rabbit and all his animal friends were getting a lot of attention as the children happily connected words to pictures, colours and numbers and so on. I let the tape play away as the children either hummed to the songs or sang as best they could.

30th March 2001

The weather was damp and downcast, like a typical English Sunday, when the best thing you can do is have a lie-in and absorb the pitter patter of the rain on the windowpanes. It seemed to have a calming effect on the atmosphere and the soul and everything was in slow motion and surreal. Patches of cloud could be seen around and under the tops of the mountain and the road works in Sirio was still in progress, making the journey to Erimi a hazardous task for the driver. The second class were expecting me to stay with them the whole three hours. I brought in two very nice videos, in which the actors were young English children with big bears and animated animals as their companions. The general emphasis was to repeat what they had learnt and to watch a story with very simple English phrases and mimes. It was as if I had waved a magic wand, just the trick. The little ones from the first class, who weren't supposed to be with me, without preamble, just wandered in and settled themselves around the television. The position of the television was just behind the door so the children were cramped around it. There were no scraps or antagonism, the rain must have produced a kind of sedative in the atmosphere. The good fairies must have made their magic bubbles and must have blown them into the air.

Mario quietly came towards me and just sat next to me without saying a word. I picked him up and sat him on the desk next to me and put my arm around him. No words were said, it just wasn't necessary. We were the best of friends again. I wondered how much affection he got or, more the case, how much he didn't get at home.

After the break I taught them how to tell the time. Adriano just couldn't be bothered. He was one of the tallest in the class and whinges a lot. Whatever movements he made, it was as if there was a great weight over his hands, holding him back. Danilo, Marina's brother was being naughty too, chatting to Alessio most of the lesson so I made Alessio swap seats with

Tommaso. Alessio suddenly screwed up his face and shouted out, 'I'm not sitting in his place, he doesn't wash!' Poor Tommaso. The children kept on taunting him, offending him, making him feel a complete nothing. Children can be really cruel. Their refusal to accept him was sharp, dispassionate and evil. Whenever Tommaso couldn't answer a question correctly, Lucianus would laugh aloud and ridicule him. The weakest and the least privileged always gets hurt and I wanted to teach them a big lesson. I purposely asked Lucianus a question which I knew he could not answer. I laughed at him and let the rest of the class laugh too.

As I drove back, scrambling up and down the ridges of Sirio with the swish of rain hitting my window screens, I contemplated my work, it was a mission, how to placate children brought up in the hidden hills of Sicily. But, they were normal children with the same characteristics as city kids, maybe city kids are more subtle in their behaviour. In the mountains everything was accentuated. If they felt angry, they were very angry, if they felt happy, they were very happy, if they were cruel they were very cruel. No doubt, Annamaria Grotti, knew what I was letting myself in for when I had accepted the job.

3rd April 2001

Every time I made my way up to the school, it felt as though I was seeing nature and its beauty for the first time. Each time there was something different, it might be the changing colours, or even the sounds, or maybe the feeling – secret sounds that you couldn't possibly detect in the middle of a traffic jam, in any city you may wish to imagine. It was just the feeling of another life around you, perhaps the nymphs were playing hide and seek and making daisy chains or just clambering over the stony walls or playing in the rushes or looking for new plants and seeds to be used as remedies for ailments.

There they were 'my kids' in the yard eating their *paninos*. Carmelita had a new hairstyle this morning, she had many miniature hairclips in her hair, even though her hair is short and wavy, as if she had been transported from the 1920s. She was always impeccable with beautiful brown eyes and spaced eyelashes like Betty Boop. She was the most intelligent girl in the school. She was standing next to me and tugged at my sleeve forcing me to bend over to listen to what she had to say. She bent her head to one side and lifted her eyebrows and holding the palm of her hands to form a secret tunnel between her sweet little lips to my ears. '*Sai, sono fidanzata con Samuel*' – 'You know, I'm engaged to Samuel.' Her big brown eyes opened wide as she watched my reaction and was excited to share such an important secret with me. I was made to feel privileged to have acquired such knowledge. 'Oh,' I acknowledged nodding my head, looking as serious as possible. I was beginning to feel like Snow White and the children I was teaching were the dwarfs. Only I don't look anything like Snow White and although they did not look like the dwarfs, all the characteristics were there.

Cettina was working well with the second class so she put her head round the door and asked me to keep the infants for the rest of the morning. By now Cettina and I had got a good understanding between us. Cettina is quite attractive and bright and in her mid-thirties. She has a modern haircut and is quite trendy too. She has one tooth missing. I was very tempted to suggest she have something done about it but thought I had better not. She had been working at the school for about six years now and knew her school kids as if they were her own. Her way of keeping discipline was quite original but it worked. She had a very loud and vibrant voice and when she thought it was necessary she used it. I didn't dare get on the wrong side of her. Hers wasn't a request but an imposition. I smiled as sincerely as I could but deep down I wanted to throw the coffee I had in my paper cup at her. Mario and Giovanni had already had their first fight, they wanted to sit on the same chair. I had planned my time equally between the two classes so now I had to think quickly of something new for the children to do. We went out to play as the sun was shining brightly. I got them to form a train and got two children to form a bridge as when you play *Oranges and Lemons*. I got each one to go under the bridge and repeat a colour, if we were doing colours and if he/she got it right, we let the child go, if not the child was trapped until she/he could remember or else he/she was out, then we went on to the days of the week, the months of the year, the parts of the body, numbers, animals etc. etc. The on-the-spot invented game was a complete success.

When I was around the age of seven or eight I remember playing a lot. I used to play when I was at St Osburg's School, I used to play in the garden, in the backyard and in Dorset Road. Televisions were still black and white and programmes did not start until the afternoon with *Bill and Ben the Flowerpot Men* and of course *Watch with Mother*. My mother didn't have a washing machine and dishwashers had not been invented yet. However, she didn't have to wash the bed sheets because there was the door-to-door dry cleaning service. I used to ride my two-wheeler bike with two little wheels on each side to help me balance well as I rode up and down Dorset Road. We lived at 27 Dorset Road and on the corner of Widdrington Road there was the corner grocery shop where my mother did a lot of her shopping and where we met all the neighbours and became very friendly with the shop keepers. The other side of Dorset Road was Somerset Road which was a long and wider road with a very old fashioned pub, probably built before the 1950s. Outside the pub there was a wide footpath which represented my playing area and for trying out my new two-wheel bike with its side wheels for support. There was an Irish family about five doors away from our house. There were about five children in this family, two of whom were twin boys. They were my age and I liked playing with them. There was also an elderly woman who lived with her cat called Arthur and she was often in her garden with her cat to keep her company. Next to us lived another widow, whom we adopted as Aunty Maudy, she was a plump and very jolly lady with very big breasts. Whenever we saw her in the garden she would be cleaning around her geraniums and clearing out the snails, once she picked one up and pretended to put it in her cleavage. My brother and I thought she had actually let it slide down her very big breasts. She often had me over for tea, apple pie and custard and every time I was over to enjoy her enormous delicious puddings I had to sit and watch the six o'clock news. The six o'clock news seemed never-ending and the newsreader was a stiff-collared man who never smiled. The pub on the opposite side of the road divided two streets with a wide footpath and that was a great spot to play in too. Along the back, outside the kitchen of our terrace house, there was a square yard and the outside toilet with the metal pull chain and heavy black seat used to be there. Next to the outside toilet there was a coal shed. Then there was a little wooden gate which opened on to the alleyway which you had to cross over into your own garden. The garden was back to back to the garden of another house over the other side. We had a little garden shed in the garden. There were two washing lines down the length of the garden held together by two poles. From my garden I could see all the neighbours' gardens and cats and dogs and bicycles. My dad had a black bicycle before he could afford to buy his first car i.e. grey mini van. He sometimes took me on his bike. He rode his bike to Far Gosford Street where there used to be a tailor's shop with a workroom. In the same street there used to be a Hospital for Dolls where my mother took me, to have my doll repaired. My doll had to be repaired because I had cut all its beautiful blonde hair when I was pretending to be a hairdresser. I used to play in my garden shed and little wooden playhouse which my dad had built. There, I played with my friends and talked to the cats. My friends were my imaginary little friends who followed me everywhere, even when I had to go to the toilet. I used to talk to them all the time and my imaginary friends had a leader who was the tallest. I imagined him to be a very lively and intelligent little man who made all the decisions for the rest of his little gang. He wore a very wide floppy hat and did most of the talking. He was the only little imaginary friend who talked to me and only became visible when I was left on my own. Further down the alleyway there was a horrible high black gate. We stayed away from that gate because we knew that in that house lived a wicked witch who cast evil spells on anybody who dared venture through her very black iron gate.

The morning was now over and I made my drive down the zigzag mountain roads – it was part of the job, manoeuvring round the sharp bends watching out for the unexpected lorries or goats or donkeys or maybe the good fairies popping out of the woods. I was thinking about the Costanzo show, which I had stayed up late to watch the night before. The discussion was about abnormal phenomena, apparently nymphs live up to the age of 400 years and they have frequent parties and when there is an eclipse of the sun, all the nymphs of the world have a big celebration and all their powers get recharged. The fairy world get together to celebrate their very existence. At every eclipse of the sun a circle is formed of the same race of the sprites and fairies. For example all the brownies of the world stand in a circle hand in hand looking towards the sky. Then all the elves of the world, stand in another circle next to the elves and form another circle, then the Pixies, then the Naiads, then the Dryads, the Gnomes, and even the Irish Leprechauns, so on and so on, just like the Coca-Cola advert when all the human race are segregated under the same sky. The fairy world travels to the place where the next eclipse of the sun will be. The next one will be in 2006 in Antarctica and all the fairy races from every corner of the earth will fly or just appear in their relative circle ready for the moment when they recharge their powers of magic. And just as the sun reappears behind the moon their faces shine happily as they feel restored and regenerated and new again. No luck this morning they didn't show up, just the odd workman or the lonely farmer on his donkey and the loud silence of the hills.

6th April 2001

It was a dull morning and quite overcast but pleasant enough as it showered gently as I drove up the beaten track. Cettina and Caterina had preceded me and were already at school sorting out the paperwork for the school lunch. The children usually give a voucher which they obtain from the Town Hall to enable them to have their free school lunch. Once the numbers are verified, it is communicated to the next village, and at lunchtime the meal van would make its way to the school to distribute their lunch packs. The school rooms then get transformed into a canteen. I had to spend three whole hours with the second class because I had spent three hours with the first class. I only had four pupils that morning because the others had decided to stay at home to rest up after their school trip the day before. Tommaso explained to me it was his very first experience on a ferry boat. He is just eight years old.

It was nice having to work with four children I was able to dedicate more time to them individually. I gave the only textbook left in my possession to Tommaso, so as not to make him feel left out or hurt his pride, I said he could borrow it. I had no intention of retrieving it and I wasn't going to tell the others either. We worked away happily at some exercises in the *Stepping Stone Book* which was about animals, a little time was spent working on the posters and then finally we watched a little of *Dr Patch*. Mario had joined in with the colouring and sat on my knee. He assured me that he hadn't done much kicking lately, in fact since Monday, moving his palms from left to right trying to calculate how many times he had hurt someone.

The day before I had to teach a class of teenagers in the city, most of whom were from middle-class families, the elite of the elite, the children who went skiing in winter and who went to exotic places in the summer and who had two homes. This particular group was quite irritating for me, not because they were full of life and mischief but because they were as dead as a doornail, passive and dull. Their responses to the lesson were mechanical and stiff, devoid of any real sentiment.

9th April 2001

It was another typical dull English day today with little light and quite overcast. Nevertheless I now felt comfortable and familiar with my journey. The bumps and bends and potholes and blind corners were now a natural feature and it didn't seem such an enormous effort to drive. I had drawn up the road map in my mind and divided my journey into three parts, and what used to seem an interminable journey, now seemed like second nature to me and a relaxing outing to go on, except of course for the 50° descent at Sirio where the diversion was still in force. The first part of the journey represented the area from my house to Ruvo, a fishing village. The second part was from Ruvo to Sirio, and the last stage of my journey was from Sirio to Erimi. I dare not blink, my brain starts cudgelling '...And if the breaks suddenly stopped working, or if there were thick, slippery ice on the steep cobbled path? It would make the path even more dangerous! What next?' Just at this point the Breil commercial on television comes to my mind where the woman goes over the slope and then into the next life. She has to choose which entrance to go through, the one leading to Hell and keep her Breil watch or take it off and choose the entrance which leads to Heaven. She decides to keep her watch on her wrist and goes to Hell. Well, my watch on my wrist wasn't a Breil, it was the watch that had belonged to my father, an Omega, not a battery watch but the original style Omega which had to be wound up every twenty-four hours. The watch was about fifty years old and it was my safety net. I knew I was being watched over by my father, and that because I wasn't wearing a Breil watch it was going to be less likely that I should end up like the attractive lady in the Breil commercial. We are all supposed to have our very own Guardian Angel and as a child I believed in this and now as an adult I would like to think that this is true and I like to think that there is an afterlife.

My grandfather, who had only one eye, had died two years before my father. I was only fifteen at the time. I was afraid of staying at home on my own thinking about my grandfather who had not long passed away. My father was angry with me for being afraid and told me that no harm would every come to me from a person who had loved me in life and if anything I would be protected. At that time my father was already suffering from Angina Pectoris and unfortunately bypass operations were not yet practised. He was a very good tailor and had, by the age of forty, made a very good name for himself. Nerelli Tailoring was the name of my father's shop which was in Radford Road on the corner of Wyley Road. Every Friday evening passers-by could see about five or six hand-made suits hanging on the clothes hangers ready to be collected. I used to assist my father in the shop when he so proudly helped his clients to choose the right cloth for the suit they wanted to be made up – made-to-measure. He took the measurements and dictated the measurements to me. I was the one who telephoned the customers to inform them to come for their first fitting, their second fitting or to remind them that their suit was ready to be collected. My father knew how to talk to his customers even though it was in broken English, he could never pronounce mountain it was always 'mointen'. He knew how to charm his customers but was never insistent. It was not necessary. Recommendation of his suit-making was done through word of mouth and gradually he had acquired a very high clientele. He could not manage all the work himself and so had to hire other tailors who were from Sicily too. At one stage there were seven people working for my father. It was a great achievement for him and my mother. Whenever the clients wanted to know about his origins he would proudly open a pack of postcards with pictures of the sea and the mountains and of Taormina. Just as my parents had reached a good position it all sadly ended when on the morning of 9th February 1972, he had terrible chest pains and suddenly died of a heart attack at the age of forty-four. My parents' dream had been completely shattered. It was a simple dream. They wanted to move to Styvechale, the posh district of Coventry. After years of hard work and struggle, it was what they deserved.

    The children seemed quite calm when I got to Erimi. I never know what to expect when I get there. Martina was now quite willing to participate in the lessons, no more tears, but Serena was in a world of her own and was fishing for my attention by saying that she didn't like English anymore. Gianpiero kept going on about his sore finger so Martina, Marina and I all placed our fingers over his swollen finger, counted to thirty and blew away the pain out of the window. Anton, the *sostegno* teacher, was there to watch over the children and I revised all the names of the animals, colours and adjectives using the flash cards. I held the flash cards up with the pictures for them to see, and then they would shout the names excitedly. They loved saying the word butterfly and cock and squirrel, cow was not their favourite word, maybe because it didn't sound such an interesting word to say. Anton then left the classroom for a while to attend to the other class. I put a poster over the blackboard which denoted the opposites of adjectives for example the opposite of beautiful was ugly, etc.

A good teacher knows when her students' concentration is focused on her or not. I felt they were losing it just then so I pretended to play a joke on Anton. I did a bad sketch of Humpty Dumpty and said it was Anton the teacher. I told the children it was our secret. So I drew an ugly Humpty Dumpty. When Anton came in the children described the ugly picture on the blackboard to him. He was impressed not realising they were describing him without him knowing.

The second class were distracted this morning because it was their first morning back at school after their school trip. I told them I was going to give them a test the next lesson so I gave them handouts of a mock test. There were three levels of ability and three different age levels so it took some thinking to get the right pitch so that all of the children could gain something positive out of this simple test. Adriano, as usual, in his pathetic disinterested way, didn't want to even attempt to look at the paper. I told them more or less what I was expecting from them, for example, the days of the week, the months of the year, simple answers to simple questions such as, 'How old are you?' etc. The next lesson with them was going to be just after Palm Sunday and I wanted to make sure that they hadn't forgotten too much of what I had taught them already before I moved on to other things. The children's minds were on school trips and festivities.

As I passed through the villages I could see palm leaves and branches in front of the doors to mark the fact that it was Passion Week, the week before Easter Sunday and Palm Sunday, the Sunday before Easter Sunday. My mind was on my lesson planning for the next week. I do a lot of thinking while I'm driving, that is once I know my way, and rummage through my mind for what to do next with the children. Although I do have my Teacher's Guide Book that goes with the textbook, it doesn't always accommodate the needs of the children as each child works at his or her own pace.

Halfway, on my journey home, I had to stop in front of one of the statues of the Black Madonna. It had its niche neatly excavated in the wall at Sirio in the back narrow lane just before reaching the stretch where the car doors cannot open. Suddenly without any ado, a butch-looking lady opened the passenger door of my car and as she made herself comfortable, asked me for a lift to Sant' Anna, one of the coastal villages. She did not wait for me to give her any answer. She just plonked herself into my passenger seat, munching away at freshly picked broad beans. I got a big whiff of vegetables, pollen and damp and the smell of earth all rolled into one. She had a wide square face with the bright blue eyes, a few missing teeth and a soft brown tanned complexion. She was wearing a pair of sandals with socks and an old brown cardigan, with lots of buttons over the front, covering her bulging stomach. At this point I had no choice but to drive along with this unknown passenger. She started talking very quickly in dialect and began to tell me her life story. She told me she had a son who was living in London managing an Italian restaurant. She went on to say that the Madonna affixed to the wall was her doing and that the Local Council had given her 5,000 lire – approximately 2,500 euros – to make the altar. She lived for the Madonna and would dream a lot and when the Madonna made her dream about numbers, she would bet on them in the national lottery. By the time we had almost reached the junction where I was to drop her off, she suddenly told me to poop my car horn and force the car that was in front of me to stop. I obeyed immediately and like the *Carry on Laughing* film, I got as close as I could safely get to the white Fiat Panda that was in front of me. There were two old men in the car with berets on their heads and white moustaches. She hardly allowed me to park the car before she had already opened the door with one big hefty left hand. She thanked me for the lift and hoped to see me again soon. Somehow I had a feeling I would see her again soon. I would be passing her home on my next trip to Erimi.

As you make your way to Erimi you see many statues of the Black Madonna. The people of this area are devoted to the Black Madonna of Tindari. Tindari is a town on the East coast of Sicily in the province of Messina but on the other side of the island. Every year in September people of this area travel through the mountains and not round the island by car. Many devotees in the past, and in the present day too, go on a pilgrimage to Tindari on foot. The villagers gather together at about three or four in the morning with very good walking shoes and make their long journey across the hills, singing and praying on their way.

10th April 2001

The children were getting used to seeing me and now every time I went up they asked me to stay with them for the rest of the day. At the age of six, seven and eight learning English is just a novelty to them, a fun thing to do, and as most of my lessons were done with games and songs I was, to them, their Mary Poppins or maybe a female version of Peter Pan. When I asked them how old I was, they would all answer together and say I was six. What they were really saying was that I was one of them. Gianpiero would just come and cuddle me and Carmelita wanted cuddling too. Maybe such familiarity with the teacher should not be allowed, but my fondest memories as a child at infant school was Mrs Branney at St Osburg's School. She was the only teacher that showed any outward affection, and every time it was home-time it was quite natural for us kids to go up to her to kiss her.

Miss James was also very nice and to this very day I can remember her saying to us, 'I wonder if you will ever remember me when you are all grown up?' I wanted to teach my Erimi kids all the objects that they used for school, i.e. ruler, rubber, pencil, satchel, glue, etc. etc. After I had fed the words to them I got my scarf and one by one I blindfolded the child and let them touch the object I put in front of them. That way they had to perceive the object with their hands and remember it in English. The game worked well because everyone wanted to have a go and every time the child guessed correctly, everybody else clapped. Then we played at *Queenie Queenie, who's got the ball, is he big or is he small, is he fat or is he thin or is he like a rolling pin?* One of the children would throw over his shoulder a small ball. One of the other children would catch it. All of them would then stand in a line with their hands tied behind their back all pretending to have the ball. This was quite hilarious because as I got them to repeat after me, I made them gesticulate, for example, as they said fat they would push their little tummies forward and when they said thin they would hold out their little finger and by the time they said rolling pin they would pretend to be using a rolling pin. Serena would have the most interesting expression. She would be perfect as an actress or in children's shows as her eyes would open wide and when she said 'fat' her little body would bend forward and her little hands would join together at the front. The children were lined up against the wall of the little class and Sabrina helped me play safely making sure the ball wouldn't break any windows. Sabrina would catch the ball and place it in one of the children's hands. The child who threw the ball had to repeat, 'Is it you?' and try and guess who had got the ball. Sabrina was also enjoying herself as she caught the ball and pretended to get excited too. We were having such fun that I had gone over my time with them.

In the second class the boys were in a scrapping mood and it's just like seeing brothers and sisters fighting over the silliest reasons. They would make friends just as quickly. Marina still had a button missing from her apron. I blindfolded Marina and got her to try and identify each class mate, asking, 'Who's he?' and for example, 'Who's got small ears?' etc. This worked quite well and because Marina was the only girl the boys didn't fight over who should be blindfolded. She felt their faces one by one with a kind of motherly touch and familiarity. She was capable of identifying each one of them and answering in English. 'He's Tommaso, he's Danilo, he's Mario.'

It was time for me to go again and Danilo and Marina packed my little Mary Poppins bags. Just as I was about to leave the classroom Mario from the other class came in and placed a note in my register with the words 'Beautiful Easter'. The paper was just a sheet ripped out from his *quaderno* without any trimmings and colours. Mario found it hard to express himself in his speech and drawings and writings but his expressions and movements made clear what he wanted to say.

I had to stop the car at the same spot again at Sirio. Up the narrow pebbled lane and left into the space where the Black Madonna lay. The Black Madonna was encased in a wall in beautiful marble with fresh flowers. I was contemplating and admiring the beautiful statue. The lady I had given a lift to, the previous lesson, suddenly appeared. She was just walking up the steps out of her kitchen door and gave me a welcoming smile.

'Buongiorno, aspetta, aspetta, ti dugno na cosa, e ti fazzu vidiri a foto di mei niputi' – 'Good morning, wait, wait, I will give you something and will show you a photo of my grandchildren,' she said in strict Sicilian dialect. Without any ado she rushed into her kitchen, making a slapping noise with her sandals, and reappeared again with a litre and a half of home-made pure virgin olive oil wrapped up in a carrier bag. I noticed again her thick socks over her sandals and it was clear that she suffered from arthritis as her big toes were bent towards the right and it would be impossible for her to wear a comfortable shoe. She came out with her photos, her son in London in a typical English house with carpets. Then another one of her pretty niece, and then another one of herself in front of her Black Madonna statue dressed in her Sunday best. I really wasn't that interested to know about what her son was doing in London. But as I had done before with the lady at the bar, I listened with great enthusiasm. It was the least I could do for the lady who had over generously given me a bottle of precious olive oil. She wanted to know when I would be passing again so that she would prepare another bottle of the local wine for me. I told her that I wasn't sure and that it all depended on my hours of work. I didn't want to appear ungrateful but I didn't want to commit myself either. I thanked her for the bottle of oil and said that it was extremely generous of her and that the oil was sufficient. She said that she liked to be generous.

I wonder if she lived in London, would she be able to stop any passer-by and get a lift so easily and if she gave away a bottle of one and a half litres of pure olive virgin oil what would the average English person do with it?

Olive oil is like butter and margarine for the English. It is used as salad dressing over salad and tomatoes. It is added to vegetables and to sauces. It is also used for frying and a lot of the locals prefer home products as they can be sure it is genuine and pure and has no additives. But it is fattening. Olive oil and black pepper spread on home-made toasted bread is just so inviting and delicious. Olive oil is easily attainable in the English supermarkets now but when I lived in England, you could only acquire it from the Continental shops or in chemists. My salads at school were served dry, like you would feed a rabbit. None of my English school friends ever knew that I had my salads at home dressed in olive oil, they would have turned up their noses. For me it was the most natural thing to have olive oil as part of my diet and even garlic, but of course I would not tell them that.

19th April 2001

Six days had passed since my last lessons at Erimi and it seemed as if I hadn't been to school for more than a month, even though the six days had gone by very quickly. The first bumpy road over the river that was, had been tarmacked over, making it easier to drive over what had once been bumpy ground. The main road in Sirio was finally open and the ground was smooth and clean. It was nice to be able to drive without having to put my driving abilities to the test. As I passed the big black statue of the Madonna I saw the same old man, whom I had seen about six times before, just standing there mesmerised by the statue. This particular statue is quite big, it is in an idyllic spot just as you have to cross over the little bridge to the other side of the mountain. The statue is protected by glass with flowerbeds in front of the statue. The Madonna looked as though it might just come alive at any moment. The man was wearing an old shabby suit with his floppy hat protecting him from the strong sunlight. To me it looked as if the man's main occupation was to walk to the statue from wherever his home was and to adore the Madonna. Everything else was superficial – all that mattered was his communication with the Madonna. The isolation of the place certainly gave it a holy feeling. It was a sacred place.

Perhaps at night the Madonna comes alive and strolls around the pretty brooks leaving a strong feeling of her presence, then just before sunlight she walks lightly on her feet with her beautiful mantle touching the ground back into her glass niche and turns back into the still statue again.

Religion is big business in Italy. It is part of the Italian culture. This does not mean that the mass population of Italians rigorously go to church every Sunday as is expected of them. To miss Mass on Sunday is a sin in the Catholic faith, well that's what I was brought up to believe in English Catholic Schools. If you go to any mass on any Sunday here you will find the worshippers are composed of elderly ladies (they seem to live to quite a ripe old age here, probably because they consume so much olive oil), a lot of mothers with their children, and quite a few men. The women outnumber the men. At Christmas and Easter and the important festivities, baptisms, confirmations, first communions and weddings, the churches are overflowing. There are not enough places in the church to accommodate everybody. You will still find the old men standing outside the church when there is a funeral and of course when there is a wedding, the women crowd around to admire and/or criticise the bride as she is taken to the church by her father.

Funerals are a sombre occasion. I much prefer the way they are conducted in England, where the idea is the celebration of life that has come to an end, whereas here the ending of a life and the separation for ever of a loved one from his or her family. Even the funerals are an interesting event. Once as I was about my business in the square when there was a funeral going on but with a band following the coffin, I thought I was seeing a scene out of a James Bond film. I was later told that the husband wanted to send his wife off into the next world in the most elaborate fashion because she had been such a good lady. Oh, I thought, quite impressed. After a moment's silence, he went on to say that the husband had had many lovers and had treated his wife badly, but whatever, she deserved a good funeral. 'Deserved' – 'meritata'. I thought to myself, if there was an afterlife I hoped she would haunt her husband to make his remaining time on earth a living misery. She deserved a good funeral. How can anyone deserve a good funeral? Did it give her the keys to heaven, was she going to get a big prize in the next life? Would she be given a trophy for being such a saintly woman?

Each village, each town, each city has its own Patron Saint that protects over its followers and *'festa'* are held annually to commemorate the saint, the Madonna or a religious event. When the statues are brought along the streets in procession they are adorned with jewellery and banknotes are pinned on the mat at the bottom of the statue. This is because the devotees had asked for a special intention and their intentions had been granted. It is their way of offering something precious to the Madonna as a thanksgiving. The *festa* are quite spectacular to watch and there is a lot of veneration and strong emotion. Pagan tradition is thrown in too which more often than not has little to do with religion at all.

Let's take the Feast of Santa Lucia, for example, which is celebrated in Savoca the second Sunday of August and 13th September. The whole village becomes an open theatre as her martyrdom is re-enacted.

In Siracusa (c.283–c.303) Sicily was under Roman rule and the Emperor of the time was Diocleziano and there was a lot of Christian persecution. A suitor found it unacceptable that his offer of marriage was refused by the beautiful Lucia. Lucia refused his proposal saying that she was already married to Christ. He denounced her to the Prefect of the city called Pascasio. Pascasio used all his persuasive powers to convince her to marry her suitor. He then ordered his soldiers to take her to the local brothel so that she would lose her virginity and become 'everybody's woman' and not belong to one mysterious God. The soldiers tried to pull and drag her from her home but she suddenly became very heavy. Bulls were used to heave her from where she was standing but even that didn't work. Then it was ordered that her eyes be eradicated. As soon as her eyes were drawn out, miraculously her face restored its natural looks again with her eyes intact. Since her martyrdom, which occurred on 13th December the shortest day of the year, Santa Lucia has become the protector of sight.

Every year a young girl of six or seven years old is chosen to play the part of Santa Lucia. Her parents have to dress her up in a beautiful white dress and she has to wear a gold necklace, which they will donate to the Patron Saint. Young men dressed up as Roman soldiers wait outside the first house of the village ready to take the little 'Saint'. They are lined up along the pebbled street pulling at a heavy rope which is then tied to two oxen. The young girl soon appears perched on the shoulder of a relative, perhaps an uncle, an older brother or grandfather, who take it in turns to carry her along the streets of the village. The other end of the rope is tied round her waist. The young girl has to sit on her relative's shoulder with her eyes downcast and her hands joined together as if she's praying. She is not allowed to look around her. I was told that the girl has to practise this the week before the procession. Then there is a loud commotion, the soldiers pull and heave from right to left then left to right, causing havoc amongst the crowd of visitors. One hefty soldier, actually stood on my toe as I was one of the spectators watching the scene. While all this is going on a man dressed up as the devil himself, all in red, wearing a wooden mask, which was made in the 1400s, skips around the girl pointing his peculiar spear towards her trying to distract her fixed gaze. The mask he wears is pretty ugly. It has two very thick eyebrows and a wide nose with a wicked smile. Two horns spring out of its head. At the end of each horn there is another ugly face. It looks as though it's smiling maliciously ready to play his ugly tricks. The spear the man is holding is rather unusual. It is not a normal spear, as at the top, it curves out like an umbrella upside down. The devil tries to distract the girl while she is solemnly praying. The devil is called '*U diavulazzu*'. He represents something quite different, not directly related to the story of Santa Lucia. He represents the satisfaction of the people when Savoca became an independent community. The young girl is carried round the village while her parents walk proudly behind her dressed up as if invited to a wedding. The statue of Santa Lucia is only put out in St Nicolas' church that day. It is a very beautiful statue made of silver. It shows Santa Lucia with a plate in her hand and her eyes in the plate. She is also holding palm leaves which are a sort of emblem to signify her courage. At the end of the procession the bulls are let loose among the crowd for a very short second. I did not wait to see this part of the spectacle.

Religious and pagan festivities all around the island are different and similar. Different because each Saint is different with a different story, the same because the people create a sort of aura as the festivities are held late in the afternoon then into the evening when the sun goes down into the deep blue sea and the stars flicker and illuminate the cocktail of colours around the village. The red sky draping over the blue sea and the green and brown landscape around the villages and of course a display of very elaborate fireworks to mark the end of the *festa*.

My morning was spent in the company of eight boys. Marina, my little helper, was not at school this morning. The naughty nymphs had placed their magic spell and there was no electricity. Oh well, by now I had got used to expecting the unexpected, the unexpected situations had now become the expected situations. A day that went smoothly from the beginning to the end was an exception not the rule. The electricity came on at 11.45 a.m. exactly. With the natural light coming through the windows we progressed with out learning. We had a nature lesson on elephants, in English of course. Elephants come from Asia and Africa and they are the biggest land animal. Then we went on to other animals describing what they could or could not do. 'Can kangaroos jump?' 'Yes they can.' 'Can birds fly?' 'Yes, they can,' and so on and so on. It was the first time we read in English together. I read first, letting them notice how different the written English was to the spoken English. Although Italian has more grammatical rules with its articles and genders, the Italian spelling is easier because it is written phonetically. For example, 'photographs' is *'fotografie'*. 'F' is 'f' and not 'ph'. The last ten minutes I played with the boys using my old tennis ball. I revised the prepositions. I hid the ball somewhere in the class and the children had to guess where I had hidden the ball. 'Where is the ball?' 'Under the table', 'in the desk', 'behind the door', 'in front of the blackboard', and so on and so on. I refused to answer unless they spoke in English. It worked very well. But boys wouldn't be boys if they didn't fight. *'Ou dissi yo a maestra'*, 'I told the teacher.' That was it. It was time for me to go again. The infants in the first class waved to me as I passed their classroom as they reminded me that it would be their turn to study English with me for the whole three hours the next time I went up.

I did not listen to the radio on my way down, I wound down the car windows and listened to the birds chit-chattering and the swish of the car wheels. I didn't see my nymphs but I knew they were there busying themselves, playing and hiding and watching me as I made my journey home.

20th April 2001

The electricity was working this morning and my infants in the first class promptly reminded me that it was their turn to have English for the whole morning, as last lesson was dedicated to the boys. The best part of the lesson is the first half hour with the very young and anything after that is just extra. After half an hour their concentration goes. A lot depends on the individual child, some are receptive and you could go on endlessly with them. Adriano, Samuel and Carmelita were easy to teach, whereas Carmela, Serena and Mario would get tired and fidgety quickly. As soon as I get the hint that their receptive system switches off I change the activity. It is as if they have a light switch at the end of a satellite dish placed on their head. The satellite dish would move around picking up the signals but would suddenly get stuck or switches itself off. It could happen any time during the lesson. Just when you think all the satellites are placed in your direction working smoothly and efficiently there is a sudden blackout. One light switches off then another and another. I have to change the activity to get all the lights switched on again. I get them to sing or play. I got them to sing *Head, shoulders, knees and toes*, which the children love to do as they try to follow my movements and sing along with me. I suddenly turn into a sort of gym teacher and my little kids copy my movements. Then we had a singsong time, the *Rainbow* song, *The farmer's in his den* and *Old McDonald*, and then Carmelita shouted, 'You promised the Queenie game because I didn't get to throw the ball.' Before my mouth started to move to make the first syllable flow out, the little infants all got up and lined themselves up against the back wall. Serena twitching, distorting her nose and puffing out at her mouth. Should she keep the habit of exercising the muscles of her face, who knows, she had the elasticity of the glassmakers when they blow into the soft glass before it takes shape. She could become a very good actress, starring in comedies. Carmelita was the brightest, the most cheerful and the most mature child in the class. She looked as if she came out of the 1920s era with a Betty Boop hairstyle, pretty and proper, not a hair out of place. Her big brown eyes with long eyelashes and hair tied back neatly with little hairpins to keep her waves in a perfect style. Her apron well pressed – a natural born princess. Even the simplest of movements were graceful and controlled. She held the ball in her hands with her face towards the blackboard ready to throw the ball over her head to her classmates. She stood next to me waiting for me to give the go ahead for the next big game, her shoulders straight and her head high, turned towards me, patient and composed – a bundle of beauty, intelligence and grace. First she had to wait for the children to sing, 'Queeniiii Queeniii whozzz got the balll. Iz he big or iz he small, iz he tall or is he short or is he like a rolling pin?' before she could turn round to guess who had caught the ball. The children mimed as they sang the song and Serena, gesticulating with her eyes, face and body, could make anybody die of laughter. She pushed her little stomach forward, blew out her cheeks as the glassmakers do, with her eyes almost popping out at the same time. The little fairies lined themselves along the edge of the windowpanes, their shadows filling the walls of the little classroom. I thought I was having hallucinations or maybe the oxygen that I was breathing had a strong effect on my brain. I watched the children intently but they carried on singing and chanting and gesticulating in a broken Coventrian accent. Whether the children could see the shadows or not I could not tell. I dare not ask them. Was I going crazy and did I need to see a doctor? No, never! I would probably get locked up and my life would never be the same again. This was my big secret and maybe one day I could recount this episode in a book and it would be up to the reader to believe me or not. Nevertheless, the game continued all through the hour until it was time for me to go. It was a sequel of movements and music echoing out into the little enchanted wood.

Once back in my home village I decided to go to the local post office to pay a couple of bills. I loathe going to any public place in Sicily. It's a nightmare. My blood pressure rises the moment I walk in the place. That's when I wish I was back in England where there is law and decorum. Nowhere in the world can beat

English civilisation. There is a race to get to the counter first. You stand there keeping watch in case some crafty person tries to push in. That infuriates me. The worst are the elderly and the well to do people. My worst experience was at this very same post office. I had been standing in, what I thought, was a queue. It was my turn to pay at the counter. I stepped forward and handed over my bills and my money under the glass guard when suddenly a little old man, who was sitting on the bench, shot up from his seat and started shouting at me. Everybody in the post office turned round to stare at me, then at the old man. I wanted to shrink into the size of the fairy I thought I had seen that very morning and fly away out of the sticky old post office. Was I going insane or was I living in an insane place? That was the big question. The little old man in his black cap had been sitting on the bench. I hadn't taken much notice of him and not for one moment did I think he was waiting for his turn in the 'queue'. I tried to be as polite as possible while trying to explain that I was next in the queue. Nobody came to my defence, exasperated, I let him pass.

People just stand about in the most disorderly fashion and you just don't know where you are in the queue. Every time I go I always ask who was the last person to come into the queue. I wait until market day when most village people are at the market looking for bargains or when there is a thunderstorm. It is normal practice to see people fighting in the village hall, post office, bank, doctor's, at the chemist and even at the bus stops. Tempers run high and there is a lot of antagonism. Italians are used to this behaviour. I am not.

Not long ago I had been to the doctor's and to my shock and surprise a ticket system had been installed. I couldn't believe my eyes. The system is quite simple just like at the National Insurance office in England. You take your ticket and when your number is up you go in. One does not phone beforehand to make an appointment either at the doctor's or at the hairdresser's. One just goes along and takes a seat. My family doctor is also the Mayor of the village and political candidate. When I eventually get into his surgery I have to try and remember what I had gone there for in the first place. As I begin to explain my problems the phone goes intermittently. My instinct is to grab hold of the telephone wire and yank it out of the wall, but then I think to myself that it wouldn't get me anywhere by doing that, so I restrain my instincts. The phone conversation ends, I manage to squeeze in my problem, he scribbles the medicine or therapy I have to take before the phone or the mobile phone starts ringing again!

Our doctor is easily forgiven. Everybody knows that his efforts and energies are towards the welfare of the villagers and the expansion and progress of the village; the building of a new swimming pool, the auditorium and general 'facelift' of the village.

24th April 2001

It was my birthday today so I thought I might celebrate it at the school with the Erimi kids. I brought some cakes made of chocolate and apricot jam. They are big and soft and melt in your mouth and if you try them with a lovely frothy cappuccino they just slide down your throat splendidly. When it's your birthday or name day, or any special occasion, people shake your hands, kiss you on both cheeks and say *'auguri'*. The word *'auguri'* literally means 'best wishes' for whatever occasion. Not like in England when you say 'Happy Christmas' or 'Happy Easter' or 'Happy Birthday' or 'Congratulations' or 'Get Well' or 'Have a Speedy Recovery'. Every little child kissed me on both cheeks and said *'auguri'* as they took their sticky biscuits and gobbled them, getting chocolate over their satisfied little faces. All 22 little Erimi kids sang *Happy Birthday* to me in the little playground. They sang *Happy Birthday* as loud as they could as they munched away while the gods and the fairies and nymphs had their own little party, singing and dancing in the woods. It was almost impossible to get into the right mood for teaching and learning so I decided to draw a picture of a whimsical clown naming the parts of the body in English. The infants drew their own eccentric clown mixing in the colours. Their combination of colour mixing could be matched to any fashion designer. I believe the influence of their surroundings helps them to develop an expert feel for colours. It was a splendid morning. What better way could anyone have a little birthday party. In the magical woods of Erimi, skipping and dancing and singing with the Erimi kids and the Erimi fairies.

26th April 2001

It was 8.35 a.m. precisely and I was making my way over the bridge in Sirio, past the statue of the Black Madonna and listening to *Speak Easy with Clive* on Radio Monte Carlo. He was explaining the word 'gonna' and then he went on to explain the meaning of 'ain't'. He plays a track from an English pop song and explains the idiomatic sense of the words. The tape is played back in the afternoon at about 2.35 p.m. and I listen to it again on my way to the other school. In the afternoon I drive down the high street of the busy city of Messina with traffic on both sides of the street. A different kind of jungle from the car journey I make in the mornings to Erimi.

I drove passed the Madonna and saw the same man I had seen the other day with his black cap in his hand and sitting in front of the Madonna in deep contemplation. When I got as far as the ramp before the little village school, the village idiot was standing still in the middle of the lane with his legs wide apart blocking my way. He stood there staring at me with his head slightly bent. I wondered what was going through his mind at that very moment and felt deep compassion for him. My car was at a 50° angle uphill and I couldn't keep the car in that position too long. He continued staring at me straight into my eyes. He had black eyes and was wearing a woollen cap which covered his forehead and stopped right in front of his eyes. His trousers were very baggy and very old and so were his shoes. A scarecrow looked better than he did. I waited a moment longer before reversing the car to drive up the alternative route. All of a sudden he started pulling faces at me. His face contorted into different expressions so that his face didn't seem at all normal any more. I couldn't help feeling just a little nervous. He was a very heavy man and there was no sign of anyone else around at that particular time. I was afraid he would start picking up the heavy logs and throw them at my car.

The children sometimes made fun of him but they always stayed at a safe distance from him, as he often picked up logs and bits of wood to aim at them. If a village idiot stood outside a village school in England the parents would protest. Here in Erimi he was part of the environment, a piece of living flesh without any goal in life. The definition of 'idiot' in the *Oxford Student's Dictionary* is 'a person with severe mental handicap'. In a lot of the villages around the coast there is a village idiot. You see them roam around aimlessly or sometimes they are in a great hurry. No matter which state of mind they may be in at that precise moment, they are impervious to the world. But to see two village idiots in one day, one becomes to wonder if it is a contagious disease. The second village idiot walks up and down the village of Ruvo, usually wearing a hat on her head. Every time I see her she reminds me of the character in the film *A Fish called Wanda*, the lady with her dogs crossing the street, who has a heart attack when her dogs get knocked over or crushed to death by some heavy concrete object.

27th April 2001

This morning I sat down in the courtyard chatting to Sabrina for a moment before the school bell was about to ring. Our conversations were quite limited to things in general, the weather and so on – just like the dinner ladies used to do when I was at St Osburg's infant school... years ago.

Serena stood about, not far from where we were sitting, and started to walk backwards and forwards making herself noticed. She put on her usual sullen expression, obviously looking for attention. At first I took little notice of her, not wanting to respond to her every whim. But inside the class, I sat on one of the desks and tried to pull her up to me. It was a daft thing to do as I nearly pulled a muscle in lifting her up – she weighed like a sack of potatoes! She put both hands to her eyes ready to rub away the tears which hadn't yet appeared from her tear ducts. She reminded me of the picture of Little Miss Muffet in the Nursery Rhyme book. Then she began to cry. Out it came her loud wailing. Her mouth opened wide and her eyes changed into two Chinese slots and her body shrunk even smaller but rounder and just as heavy. '*Che cos'hai?*' (What's the matter?) I asked. Now what! The morning lesson hadn't yet begun and here I was acting as mummy again. '*Mario mi ha chiamata* ——*!*' ('Mario has just called me a ——!') Like Mary Poppins, I walked out towards the courtyard with Serene's hands clasped into mine. Mario was still happily eating his chocolate batch with chocolate spread across his mouth. He had a new haircut which made his crystal clear light blue eyes sparkle even more. I scolded him hard as he tried to justify his misbehaviour. Nowadays you are not allowed to spank the children in the schools. It is against the law. I personally think there is no harm in it. I got punished at infant school many times for lesser crimes. I remember the teachers used to get the children and slap them across the legs or hands, or even make them stand or kneel in the corner for half an hour. He certainly deserved to be spanked but all I could do was make him apologise to Serena and promise not to use such bad words again. I thought he would protest and I was ready to turn nasty on him. He just simply looked at her for a second and gave her a sloppy hard kiss on her wet cheek, then, he lifted up Serena's arm and got her little finger to bend, then he hooked his little finger round hers. Then he said something incomprehensible to her in his muffled dialect. Whatever he said Serena certainly understood him. Serena's sulky face turned into a happy smile. I wondered if my mission in Erimi was to teach English or to teach little humans to be civil. Dealing with unruly children with speech impediments did not come into the teacher training session for teachers of English, nor does teaching English to children with autistic problems. Later on in the subsequent year I taught a class with a child with autistic problems; it is quite possible to teach English as a foreign language to a child with autistic problems. They have quite a good memory, but of course only when you have them on a one-to-one basis.

It was Friday and who likes working on a Friday with the weekend in mind? The boys' minds were concentrated on what they were going to do after school. Attending to their animals, pigs and donkeys, dogs and cats, rabbits and even birds, playing in the brooks and hills, and watching TV. It is an imposition to be stuck in a classroom surrounded by hills and birds singing sweetly. It was certainly not conducive to learning English or any other subject for that matter. As you look out of the window, it is as if the sun or God has sprayed rays of sunbeams onto the hills. An artist could not make the blending of the greens and greys along the slopes of the hills more precise. I wanted them to listen to a simple recording in English and to repeat it. It was the most I could get them to do and no way could I blame them for not wanting to study. The boys' good behaviour lasted just over half an hour – and that was a miracle. The light rays penetrated into the class. The Pixie behind the windowpane had thrown a mischievous spell into the little classroom, just as if he had thrown talc into the air for the children to breathe. It was contagious. One joker changed the speed of the voice on my recorder and the instant I turned my head round another untied my bootlaces. So, I decided to teach them a lesson. I switched off the tape recorder, put my books away and started to get ready to go.

I wanted them to feel guilty for playing tricks on me. I was offended with them. There was silence. The Pixie hiding outside behind the glass pane shrugged his shoulder with his little cap nearly falling off his head. I could see him and was observing him from the corner of my eye. He must have been about five inches tall. His cap was pointed at the top and was a brilliant red. It looked hand-made with cross-stitches across the centre of it. Next thing I saw him pulling a face. He stretched out his already cross-eyed eyes with his very long fingers. His hands were quite small and slender but his fingers were very long and bony. His nose was pointed at the top and had quite wide nostrils. He was laughing wickedly with his long and wet tongue stretched out. He was wearing a dark greyish, ragged T-shirt with matching shorts. His knees were bony too. He wore boots that seemed as old as the Pixie himself. The boots were pointed at the end and turned upwards at the top and they didn't have any soles or heels. They seemed made by hand too, with cross-stitches along the top near the knee. His ears stuck up and out from his head, just like donkey ears. They were moving constantly. He crossed his eyes at the centre, just like a naughty young child would do.

Alessio, the older of the boys got up, 'No teacher. *Scusa, scusa, non lo facciamo più.*' 'No teacher. Sorry, sorry, we won't do it again!' I continued to act offended and insisted that I didn't want to teach them any more. Alessio got up from his desk and put his arm around me, so did Danilo and before I knew what was happening the boys had trapped me in their circle. They all held hands and wouldn't let me go. The bond was intense and I was dumbstruck.

There are few words to describe that magic moment, me and my Erimi kids. I sat down again, they sat down with their hands folded not saying a word. I opened my tape recorder and we started to repeat and sing along to the song as best we could in English. Harmony was restored. I had won my battle with the Pixie, the Fairies were on my side and their magic was stronger than that of the Pixie.

I reversed my car to go home and the old man standing on the balcony waved and smiled at me, I waved back but would have quite happily stayed there for the rest of the day. I drove down and around the bends, listening to the birds twittering away as my car silently swished by. The pigmies, pixies, elves and nymphs were busying themselves and playing in the woods – a penetrating, loud silence sweetly blending in the wind.

30th April 2001

Today I decided that the children should revise the colours, animals and numbers in English. Repetition is indispensable for anyone learning a second language. I got out my flash cards of animals, numbers and colours and taught the children to play snap. Mario put down his card which was a picture of a squirrel but he did not say snap quickly enough. Serena, who also had a picture of a squirrel in her hand, slammed down her hand and shouted snap. Mario got up very angry with himself and went over to the other side of the room and started crying. Carmela, put her arm around his shoulder to placate his temper. I didn't take any notice of his little tantrums and encouraged the children to carry on without him. Just then, Anton, the *sostegno* teacher came in. I was quite cross with him too, because the next thing he did was to try and humour Mario out of his bad temper. Then we had a singsong of *Head, shoulders knees and toes*. To impress the children, and so that they would remember the parts of the body I got them to draw round their hands and feet in their copybooks and write the words inside their drawing. It seems such an elaborate process just to learn English words, but it works, especially with the very young. When the children started taking off their shoes, the scent of smelly feet was overwhelming. Mario decided to pull his patchy sock off and we all looked at his grimy foot. It was an awesome spectacle! Serena and Carmela turned up their little noses and Carmelita squinted her eyes as if the sight might damage her sight.

   I repeated the exercise with the older group, and as they drew around their hands and feet they gossiped amongst themselves. Gianpiero was telling his classmates about his meeting with his friends from Casale.

   Casale is another forlorn village high on a hill top. His friend had boasted that he could count to ten in English. Gianpiero told him to '*A cucati!*' literally, 'Go to bed!' which means that what you're saying is not at all impressive. In fact, it's quite boring.

Gianpiero told his friend that his English teacher made his class count up to 100, so that of course meant that his English teacher was much better.

It is quite interesting and comical to watch these wonderful children in conversation. It is like watching grown-up people in young bodies discussing the simple things of life. A bit like watching dwarfs, in a way, but of course these are real children. Their upbringing is definitely unique but may not always be to their advantage. When Tommaso was asked what he wanted to do when he grew up he simply said he wanted to stay in Erimi all his life!

6th May 2001

Red poppies and wild plants of deep purple spilling about along the mountains is a pretty background for any artist to paint, as they move to the music of the wind. When the sun shines everything comes alive and the plants look as if they are chatting and dancing with each other as they sway about in the wind. Driving up to Erimi was a magical trip to fairyland and I enjoyed my drive every time. I had only six boys to teach this morning so I thought I would have an easy time, especially now there was an understanding between us. But no, it was impossible for them to be pleasant. However, this morning they were trying. It didn't last very long, though. I got them to copy down verbs from the blackboard and made little flash cards with them. Then I put all the flash cards mixed together on the table and divided the boys into two groups. I wrote a sentence on the board such as 'Kangaroos can't climb.' First I got them to repeat it and tell me in Italian what it meant. Only when they got it right I started the quiz. 'Are you ready?' 'Yes,' they shouted at the top of their voices. 'Go!' And like a game of scrabble they had to find the flash cards as quickly as they could putting them in the same order as I had written on the blackboard. '*Vinciu yo,*' shouted Danilo, then Alessio argued. 'NO, *Vinciu yo!*' Literally translated, 'I won', 'No, I won', and so on and so on. The pushing and shoving started, and I had to stop their squabbling before it got any worse.

Italians cannot accept defeat. You see this when the football players are beaten in a football match. If they are beaten it's a big disgrace and they are jeered at by the crowds – and if they have been defeated in a European or World Championship – they have to put up with the crowds throwing insults at them and it is quite a foul attitude. However, I do agree when they are accused of getting a high pay packet for kicking a ball around the pitch. It's cynical of me I know, but football to me means big business, not sport.

I changed the exercise and by giving them different phrases to write I avoided giving them the element of competition. Anton suddenly appeared, and hearing the children arguing he started shouting himself. They of course took little notice.

Sicilians are used to shouting or speaking in a loud voice, so are the Italians from northern Italy, for that matter. They like to be theatrical. It's quite normal to see people arguing. You can be driving along minding your own business and you may see two people arguing about a minor car crash or even just shouting at you for being careless in the way you drive, or if you are in a restaurant the waiter may serve somebody else first. You can see a really interesting battle at the post office, because some smart— tries to push in, or if you like, watch two people in a heated conversation along the street, or even while waiting to go to the toilet. Italians just l o v e to argue. And when they argue their hands and arms go all over the place, and their eyes almost pop out of their heads. They also love to be spectators. The pixies and the fairies of Erimi also love to argue too. Except the fairies never get hurt because as they get hit they just flitter up into the air and laugh at their adversaries. Every time the Erimi kids get into a tiff the pixies stand behind the window and take sides cheering their favourite classmate. And because Daniel was the smallest in the class, he had a little fan club going in the world of the fairies, and for as long as he lives, he will never know.

8th May 2001

Annamaria Grotti phoned me to tell me that she wanted to divide my teaching time to include the infants from Play School – what they call '*Materna*'. I was not at all enthusiastic about the idea because it meant me teaching very elementary things to little more than toddlers and I knew it would be hard work. However, I could now officially say that my teaching had turned full circle as far as teaching English as a second language to people of all ages, was concerned. In the Language School in Messina my oldest student was 80 years old and my youngest in Erimi was three years old.

The 80-year-old was a retired surgeon who had had a serious operation to his head in Scotland. His objective was to learn English as best he could so that he could go back to Scotland to thank the surgeon who had operated on him. He was a very jolly person showing a lot of enthusiasm. This is very important for the teacher. His age was not an impediment to his acquisition of the language. I had a lot of admiration for him. On that same course, I had students who were his grandchildren's age and in comparison they were quite blasé. Another interesting observation was that the reaction to getting the language right from an infant and from an elderly person was almost the same.

11th May 2001

Plans were being made to use the school as a voting centre, so the school was going to shut for two days. The children were looking forward to having a long weekend at home. I couldn't blame them at all. It's not easy for the children in the south to study. The schools in Sicily generally start around 23rd September. Sicily is the last region in Italy to start the academic school year. This is because of the very hot summers. As a consequence the terms seem long and tedious. Children have to do so much homework and they have to memorise almost everything they have learnt in the classroom, and they also have to attend school on Saturdays too. Apart from the Christmas break lasting three weeks, and Easter, lasting only one week, there are no other breaks except for the odd national holiday or feast day.

But of course, when summer comes the children have a school holiday of almost three and a half months to look forward to. They usually break up around 10th June and start the new school term around 25th September. School starts much later in Sicily because of the incessant heat. They also have to go to school on Saturday mornings, so they don't get much of a weekend. They have lots and lots of homework to do. Quite a few go to swimming lessons, karate lessons, dancing or music lessons. So the children are kept busy. Six weeks is what I had when I was growing up in Coventry. I much prefer the British system, with frequent breaks during the school year.

In the long summer months, the children who live near the sea spend a lot of time at the beach. But for the Erimi kids it might not always be possible. The alternative for them is to get involved with their family activities and get together in the village square to play and chat and to participate in the summer festivals – or have their own little adventure in the woods.

Twenty hours of my 120 hours were to be allocated to the infants so I had to divide my time between three different classes.

It was decided that we would do an end-of-year play,

involving the two primary classes and including the infants. Looking back now as I write this 'diary' of events, I realise what a big enterprise I had taken on.

We decided to invent a story based in the little village of Erimi so I let the children shout out their ideas. Marina helped me to write out the script. We wrote it first on the blackboard so that the whole class could see their ideas being formed. As all ten children of my second class were to be included, a part had to be invented for every single one of them. I had to make sure that each child had to say no more than a line or two. Their little world in Erimi was made up of their grandparents, their uncles and aunts, their parents, and their friends. The story was very simple.

One day one of the little boys goes missing, little Tommaso of course. Alessio set the scene of the story. He was the most imaginative of them all and suggested the mother and father were working their land when they realise their little son Tommaso is nowhere to be seen. They start to get anxious. They start to phone around in the little village, their parents, brothers and sisters and friends and cousins, asking if Tommaso was thereabouts. Marina was going to dress up as the grandmother with a big white apron round her waist and flour in her hair. That way she would look old like a grandmother is expected to look. We had to make the noise of the phone and each child had to say that they hadn't seen Tommaso. 'He's not here' – 'I haven't seen him,' etc. etc. until the end when they all shout out, 'Where is Tommaso?' Tommaso then springs up behind a bus made of cardboard and shouts out at the top of his voice, 'Here I am! Here I am!' It took me a long time for me to get him to say it right because he kept on repeating, 'Hear ham.' Old wallets were used as telephones.

I found the kids from Erimi were very resourceful. Before the actual day of the presentation of the play they went to a lot of trouble to draw a beautiful tree on an old box. I was sceptical at the time whether all would come out at all well. To blend the colours of the tree they had got the different colour chalks and scratched the chalks with a knife. The powder which fell off the chalks was then rubbed into the cardboard box to make the abstract effect of the browns and greens. They had got another discarded box from one of the shops and flattened it. Then they covered it with a very wide sheet of paper and drew an old-fashioned bus. The bus was to be held up in place so that Tommaso could hide behind it and pretend to be asleep in it. Soft tissue paper was cleverly placed around the branches to give a twilight effect. The background was going to be quite elaborate too. A big sun and a lovely big rainbow. Just perfect, as the children were going to sing the *Rainbow* song too.

16th May 2001

I had few lessons to teach now and was looking forward to a well-earned rest. I had been teaching in Erimi in the mornings and in Messina in the afternoons, and there was a fair bit of driving to do in between lessons. You tend to lose yourself as your energies get depleted. Your time and patience are given to people and when you see so many pupils and students in the same day, exhausting is an understatement. You have to really like working with people and have to have the art of being able to deal with different characters. Yes I call it art or it can be defined as a special gift.

The children of Erimi slowly 'grow on you' – maybe it was because there were only a few children compared to an ordinary city school, or maybe because we were out there in the magical woods together to share the enchantment of the place and there was a special silent incantation in the atmosphere. The quiet whisperings of the fairies and of the trees in the wind. And when it gets hot you can feel the spirits of the gods, the Cyclops and even the ancestors of the different races floating around in the spaces between the trees and the brooks and secret hiding places.

The children were now used to seeing me and the moment I got into the school they would insist I stay the whole day. They had no concept of time, of obligations and appointments. Theirs was a free spirited attitude towards life. They didn't live in cities, where the passing of cars, buses and trams, gives the impression that people are going somewhere, when in truth they are going nowhere at all. The kids of Erimi were oblivious to the rest of the world. Their world was real and they had all their territory to themselves.

It was nice. With very young children you know where you stand, no pretences. Children say what they really think, and you don't expect any surprises in the end. There was now a healthy contest going on between my two classes. The children kept tags on how long I stayed in each class.

My little assistant Marina was there to sort out the gang and she helped me distribute the script for the end of year play. We sat in a circle and we started to practise the lines. I got the boys to repeat their parts in perfect Coventrian English – yes it was going to be a great show!

17th May 2001

As soon as I got into my infants class I knew it was going to be a hard morning. I knew I had to get the children ready for 8th June, the big finale and I felt I was not going to pull it off. I didn't want to disappoint the parents or the headmistress. And as soon as I saw Mario I knew he was going to pull some trick or two. Little Carmelita pulled at the side of my sleeve and showed me the nursery rhyme book with the picture of a baby in a basket up in a tree. She wanted to learn the *Rock-a-Bye Baby* song. I said it would be quite a big thing to recite it in English and that maybe we could write it down and she could read it in front of the parents. She insisted she would learn it by heart.

We decided she would hold a doll in her arms and rock the doll as she recited *Rock-a-Bye Baby*. I wrote the song down as if written in Italian so that she would get the accent right.

Suddenly, for no reason, Cristofaro went for Carmela and thumped her forcefully on the back. Poor little Carmela. She was the daintiest of them all with a pretty little face with blue eyes and blonde hair. Her tears came rushing out and quite understandably too. There was no reason why he should thump her. I got very angry with Cristofaro and was very stern and nasty with him. He started to cry and shrivelled up in the corner of the class sobbing his heart out. I insisted that nobody should go to him to humour him. His sobbing stopped and then he sat in a sulk. Having sorted him out Gianpiero started crying, with his eyes screwed up and lost in his skull, he crouched on the floor pressing his hands to his stomach. His sobbing changed into an insufferable lament. I wanted to yank him by the feet and throw him out of the windows to the Cyclopes living over the other side of the mountains at the foot of Etna. Cristofaro was still sulking with his head down and his arms folded. Little Mario went up to Cristofaro and put his arm round Cristofaro's shoulders to comfort him.

My determination to be unforgiving didn't last very long. In the end I took Cristofaro to me and just said, 'All right, let's be friends.' I turned round again to sort out Gianpiero when from behind Cristofaro came up and hugged me hard and gave me a kiss. The children were getting excited about the school presentation, especially the fact that it was to be in English, which made it even more special. I could now see it all in my mind, the cardboard tree with the cradle in it, the bus, the cardboard clock.

The cardboard clock was going to be used so that two of the infants could recite the *Hickory Dickory Dock* song. Oh what a great show it was going to be!

It was already quite hot, it was 30° but nice. The nymphs and the pygmies were also getting excited about it all. I could hear them play and sing in the woods as I swished past.

21st May 2001

It wouldn't be long before the end of my adventure at Erimi. I had very mixed feelings. There was a bond between us and whatever happened after, the building of the new school, the children growing up – that time in Erimi had been given to us – a gift from the heavens.

I was sitting in the courtyard watching the children eating their extraordinary breakfasts. Danilo pulled a cord out of his pocket. Whatever else he had was a big guess as his pocket was very bulky. I guess he had very big marbles, nuts, and sweets and miniature picture cards with his favourite footballers printed on the front. I asked him to give me the string and tied the two ends. I showed the kids how to make a shape of a spear from this piece of string. '*Voglio farlo io*', '*Anch'io*' – 'I want to do it', 'Me too'. And so with great patience I got the cord and held it around my two hands and with my middle finger I picked the string from the other hand and made the shape. One by one they tried to do it themselves without making any knots. Only Marina managed in the end, and the boys were pretty cross about that too. It wasn't possible that a girl should be able to do such a technical thing before the boys could.

We walked into the class and the first thing that Carmelita did was come to me with a very elaborate picture. It was like a Fairy Godmother and Mary Poppins rolled into one with delicate colours of pastel blue and pink holding an umbrella and a magic wand. With her big brown eyes and her magical smile she said '*Sei tu*' – 'It's you'.

If only, I thought. I was mesmerised by the picture. I sat looking at it for a moment and was amazed at how she had portrayed me. The Fairy Godmother was slim and tall with a very young face. She obviously didn't see the real me. Not very tall, slightly round, a round face with brown eyes and brown hair. One month in a beauty farm would not be enough to get my body into shape again. Well, let's say it would be better than nothing and a private PE trainer to help me get into shape would be quite nice too. Maybe what happened was that every time I passed the borders from the real world to the hidden little village of Erimi my body made a transformation. I became young and dainty and tall AND perfect. Maybe the fairies did one of their magic touches on me too without me realising it. Maybe the children did not see the real me, they saw Mary Poppins, young and slim and pretty and fresh. *'Veramente sono io?'* – 'Is it really me?' I said. She smiled and for an instant she did not answer and simply said, *'Certamente sei tu'* – 'Of course it's you!'

23rd May 2001

What a typical misty downcast English morning. The mist and cloud mingled together giving a surrealistic feeling. The journey now didn't seem nearly as long, as by now I had memorised every pothole, cranny and brook. As I drove past the Square in the village of Sirio, a group of men were taking out the carriage which was to be used to carry the statue of the Black Madonna. There was going to be a procession and a '*festa*'. The weather did not dampen the enthusiasm and expectation of the locals nor of the children at the school of Erimi. On the contrary, it had a mellifluous effect. I felt it too.

Mario and Gianpiero were absent this morning. The morning was spent rehearsing. We sang the *Rainbow* song, 'Red and yellow and pink and green...' and with every word the children bowed their little heads and every time I opened my eyes wider and rocked my head to the tune of the song so did they. Little Martina the cry-baby had finally decided to participate with the other children. Her tantrums had only recently stopped and it now didn't seem normal to see her behave as a normal child again. Everything was running smoothly, it seemed too good to be true. I was able to help the children and the more we repeated the nursery rhymes and the play the better they became at it. It wasn't going to be an embarrassment after all.

It had been decided that the 4th, 5th and 6th June rehearsals were to be held in Misinga, the nearest village to Erimi. The school there was bigger and better equipped. There was a very big classroom with a big television and lots of toys for the children. As you enter the building there is a big hall used for assembly and for voting.

My last four days of going up and down the mountains of Erimi was very pleasant. The days got hotter and hotter and light sparkling through the trees got brighter and brighter, and the birds' singing got louder and louder. Now and then I would miss a black rattle snake cutting across the paths of the winding roads and with Freddy Mercury singing, 'What a Beautiful Day', his voice mixing in with the singing of the birds and the rustling of the leaves. The fairies and the nymphs were happy too as they danced round and round holding hands, skipping and jumping and laughing and giggling in anticipation of the great show.

The children broke the silence of the building when they arrived at Misinga. They sat in the big class with the big television to have their breakfast. There were thirty seven children in all, brothers and sisters and cousins and uncles and aunts. The future generations. The family clans sat together. The little brother with the big sister, all dutifully caring for each other making sure that each one had had enough to eat.

Sometimes people say, 'Act your age' or 'Don't be childish'. Children can be more mature than adults and why we label people's behaviour by saying they are childish, I really don't know. Why does society have to categorise people like other beings. In the fairy world and in the little world of Erimi these rules do not apply.

We all went into the hall after breakfast to put everything together for the last time.

8th June 2001

The morning of 8th June was now a reality. Like the date of the wedding day or the big exam, or the opening night of a new show. The children were excited and nervous. They had learnt their lines and songs and nursery rhymes. The question was would they forget it all when the moment came for them to perform for their family and friends? And most of all for the Headmistress. There was just enough time for one more rehearsal and the final touches to the scenario. The rainbow, which had been drawn onto a semicircle of cardboard, was pinned on to the black curtain and 'The Erimi Kids' was written over it in big yellow letters. The tree, the big bus and the giant clock were on the little stage. They were neatly put to the side ready to be used. The poster of the members of the Royal Family was put up on the walls and also postcard pictures of England. A little bit of England in the midst of the hills of Sicily.

'Good. *Bravi! Adesso ripeti ma più forte. Guardate i vostri amici e genitori quando cantate o recitate – non con gli occhi in giù*' – 'Good, now repeat, but a little louder. Look at the audience when you sing or recite not with your eyes down,' I said. '*Non pulire il naso*' – 'Don't pick your nose,' rattled on Cettina. '*Adesso andate a mangiare e indossate i costumi*' – 'Now go and have something to eat and then put your costumes on.'

One might have thought that Poseidon, god of the sea and earthquakes was walking around. The pounding of their little feet as they jumped off the little wooden platform to gobble up their breakfast made the hills quiver.

I was now their make-up artist. The boys were quite still as I delicately painted their moustaches and wrinkles on their faces. Talc was scattered into their untidy hair to try and make them look old. It was like getting the kids ready for a little pantomime. Adriano was to act as the grandmother. He quite proudly produced his sister's big sized bra with lots of cotton wool. They had thought of everything. I clipped on his bra and stuffed as much cotton wool into the cups, and what a transformation! The wrap-over apron, the glasses, the handkerchief over his head and a walking stick in his hand. He was truly comical.

The troupe footslogged into the hall, the little makeshift theatre. Big tables were placed against the back wall, with a whiter than white cloth on the table, for the parents had decided to bring their home-made cakes and refreshments. The little wooden chairs were placed in a row one after another. Mothers and babies and big brothers and aunts and uncles sat in their Sunday best. It might have been a Weight Watcher's club as I had never seen so many fat people gathered in one place all together, their fat bums overlapping the little wooden chairs and their faces round as a fried egg with big brown eyes and brown hair. The mothers wore make-up, mainly red lipstick and stacks of powder on their faces. It was very hot and the wafts of perspiration from their hairy flabby arms, disinfectant, talc, aftershave and stale perfume mingled nicely in the air. There was no air conditioning, so the windows were left open, allowing the flies to float in. This hot and sticky atmosphere caused me discomfort. Was it all worth my while? It would only last about twenty minutes. Just like preparing for an elaborate meal. The time, the effort, the ingredients, all eaten up in about twenty minutes.

We waited and waited and waited and… The children shuffled and whispered and shoved each other and pulled faces. They were gradually getting bored and tired. Adriano and Mario soon got into a scrap. A really good one. I had to climb up the platform to separate them. Adriano's breasts had moved from horizontal position to vertical position. Mario started crying and wouldn't stop. He was about to get into his usual sulk so I got Serena to calm him down. She was the only little human being who could humour him.

On the windowpane, the youngest fairy of only seventy years was watching the scene. She can't have been more than three centimetres tall. She had the prettiest little face I had ever seen in my life. The colour of her eyes was of a delicate crystal blue which sparkled in the light. Her hair was long to her ankles but not straight across her shoulder but floating all over the place as she managed to stay in the air. She had a lovely dress just like a ballet dancer's. It was of a soft yellow and gold and in layers like petals around her little body. All around her body there was a light, a kind of protective barrier encasing her in her little space. Her wings flittered above her, too fast to see clearly. She was covering her eyes with her little hands with her fingers spread out. She must have thought the whole thing would end up in a fiasco. The chairs the families were sitting on, seemed to sway from one side to the next. My vision of the little chairs slowly cracking apart was getting quite vivid.

The other nymphs and fairies, on the watch out in the woods, had spotted her, Annamaria Grotti was driving round the last bend before reaching the school. She whizzed passed in her white Fiat, screeching round the bends. She reminded me of Supergran but dressed like a much younger version of the Queen Mother, in a brightly coloured dress. She was a kind of a welfare officer and home affairs minister put together. Her elegant posture impressed the locals and when she walked though the main doors she was warmly welcomed by the teachers and the caretakers. The Deputy Mayor was also there which made the meeting even more officious.

Another long never-ending twenty minutes passed by and the children were doing their best to be on their best behaviour. By now they had quietened down. Annamaria Grotti and I hadn't met since the morning she had brought me to the school. At that time I was a mysterious stranger to the children, and here I was now, six months later, completely and wholly part of them. 'The Erimi kids'.

The parents sat down on the little chairs, the teachers stood to one side of the hall. Annamaria Grotti and the Deputy Mayor sat in the first row. The nymphs and the fairies were peeping through the cracks of the windows with their tiny little eyes wide open.

The toddlers sat in their places in a circle on the floor at the foot of the stage and my Erimi kids were in position on the stage ready to start. The infants had coloured paper bibs round their necks as they represented the wild flowers in the woods. Isabella, who was blonde with light blue eyes was wearing a pretty pink frock, which caught everybody's attention.

'Are you ready?' I shouted. 'YEEEEEEEEEEEEEEEEEESS!' my Erimi kids shouted back. 'One, two, three…'

'Red and yellow and pink and green, orange and purple and blue, I can sing a rainbow...' And as they sang they rocked from right to left and left to right, moving their little heads like puppets on a string. Sometimes their little heads would go the wrong way and they would accidentally bump their heads together. The baby infants walked in a circle as the rest of the children sang. One of the children's shoes slipped off and almost caused a crash. At the end of the song I called each baby infant by their name, 'Eliza.' Eliza stood up looked for her mother in the hall and shouted in Coventrian English, 'I am a flower.' Then I called, 'Cosimo.' Cosimo stood the moment Eliza sat down again and shouted out as loud as he could, 'I am a yellow petal.' The infant teachers were delighted and so was I. We glanced over to each other and knew that it was going to be all okay. Then came *Old MacDonald had a farm* and Serena was the centre of attention as she dutifully sounded out all the animal noises. Then *Rock-a-bye Baby*, and then *Hickory Dickory Dock* and so on until at long last the grand finale. The school play. 'And where is he?' 'Is he with you?' were the first opening lines of the script. Alessio put on his worried grandmother look and pretended to phone around the village to put out the alarm that Tommaso was missing. Even though they shouted out their simple English phrases, it was a big achievement for them. They were acting and speaking in English. What a scene! The last line was said by Tommaso. 'Here I am,' he shouted as he jumped up behind the bus. Not 'hair I ham' as I thought he would say. And even if it had come out that way who would have known the difference. 'Clap, clap, clap, clap, clap.' The clapping went on and on and the children bowed and bowed until Annamaria Grotti got up from her seat. All the noise and the shaking stopped. Silence. The nymphs and the fairies were still clapping and jumping up and down but nobody had taken any notice of them. Except for me. I was staring at them. Just like in the movie films when all the noise around you is suddenly not noise but just quiet and you are not really there any more. And you are observing all the scene from a completely different dimension. Hypnotised.

Annamaria Grotti made her speech. Everybody clapped. Then she turned to me and asked me to make a speech too. I stood there immobile, trying to find something intelligent to say. I couldn't say anything. Nothing came to mind. I looked around me wishing that I could just suddenly disappear. Annamaria coughed a couple of times and stared hard at me. She was mentally communicating to me to say something and to snap out of it quickly. I took a big breath and said what a wonderful experience it was to work with the Erimi kids. I made my comments sound as sincere as possible. All I could think of was that it was finally over and that my lessons with the children would remain a very sweet memory – like a magic existence in the magical hills high above the clouds. My voice broke. I couldn't say any more. My little kids. My Erimi kids started clapping and cheering. Everybody joined in.

We ate and drank and chatted for the remaining part of the morning until it was time to go. One mother whispered in my ear that she wanted to meet me afterwards, a little way down the road where her car was parked.

I went to every single child and said goodbye, not knowing whether I would ever see them again. It was a very difficult and emotional separation and so I promised that I would return to visit.

I had parked my car a little way down the lane. Marina's mother gave me a very beautiful plant with a thank you card from all the parents of the children I had taught.

The pretty plant was quite big and it took up most of the space on my back seat of the car. I needed to leave. I felt quite sad and didn't want to show my true emotions.

I drove slowly this time past the brooks and bumpy hills. No music, just the sound of the wheels and the engine against the natural sounds of the birds and rustling of the leaves. I was completely lost in my thoughts and was going over in my mind the events of the day and of the last six months. It was now all over. I looked into the rear mirror to check that the plant wasn't wobbling too much, when I thought I saw the leaves flickering. The greens of the leaves were changing colours from light green to dark green, and within its various shades of green. I had not seen so many different shades of green before. I slowed down and thought that I had had too much to drink and eat and that I was seeing things. I stopped the car to adjust the plant on the seat better. I didn't want it to fall on its side. I had convinced myself that I was just imagining the leaves changing colours. I switched on the engine and continued my journey down the path. I looked into the rear window and this time it was the petals of the flowers. They were white Camellia. The petals started to change colour, first white, then less white then yellow then white again, then a brilliant white. I stopped the car for the second time and checked that the plant was okay. It looked quite normal. I got back into the car and thought I had better get home soon and sober up.

I took the plant into my garden and left it on the patio floor just outside my living room. It was a very big plant and I decided that I would plant it straight into my patio flowerbed.

A month had passed by since I had left Erimi. I was watering the plant one morning and tidying the leaves. There right in the middle of the plant what should I find…?

Printed in the United Kingdom
by Lightning Source UK Ltd.
107662UKS00001B/188